Ruth

Gleaning the Fallen Sparks

Ruth

Gleaning the Fallen Sparks

Rebbetzin Chana Bracha Siegelbaum

Midreshet B'erot Bat Ayin
Holistic Torah for Women on the Land

Ruth: Gleaning the Fallen Sparks רות—ליקוט הניצוצות הנפולים

Published by Midreshet B'erot Bat Ayin: Holistic Torah for Women on the Land
Text Copyright © 2014 Midreshet B'erot Bat Ayin

COVER ART: Elisheva Shira
GRAPHIC DESIGN & TYPESETTING: Ruth Simchi

Midreshet B'erot Bat Ayin
The Village of Bat Ayin
Gush Etzion 90913
Israel

Tel: 972.2.993.2642
Fax: 972.2.993.1215
Email: info@berotbatayin.org
www.berotbatayin.org

ISBN-13: 978-1497528666
ISBN-10: 1497528666

Printed by CreateSpace, An Amazon.com Company
Available on Kindle and other devices

To order additional books, please email **info@berotbatayin.org**

Dedications

*T*his book is dedicated with love to the memory of my grandmother Tzesne (Tilda) Vainer whom I didn't merit to really know, as she passed away when I was four, 24 Nissan 5725 (April 26, 1965). I do remember that we called her the Yiddish name for grandmother, Bubbe and that she was a true Bubbe in every way. My father always speaks so fondly about his Yiddishe Mamme. She was full bodied, kind and an incredible cook in the Yiddish way. She was an exceptionally talented seamstress, who sewed me a special little red jacket with so much love. I remember her warmth with which she always welcomed us, and how she would take me on her lap to check if the skin on my thumb was still all wrinkled from sucking it. If not, she would reward me with a sugar treat. My Bubbe is my only direct link to a Jewish woman of the old world who dedicated her entire life in service of others. She would cook, bake, sew, mend and take care of everyone. She is indeed a role-model of a true Yiddishe Mamme.

*C*ontinued blessings and success to Midreshet B'erot Bat Ayin.
- The Churgin Family

*D*edicated to Midreshet B'erot Bat Ayin and the holy work of all those who strive toward self-transformation.
- Judith B. Josephs

L'*ilui Nismat* Tzirel bat Rivka whose memory continues to support and inspire me.
- Mindy Sarah

L'*ilui Nismat* our beloved mother Chaya Janna Yveguenia bat Yosef & Lucia Clara. May her soul rest in Peace in Gan Eden.
- Ariela Ayoun

L'*ilui Nismat* Devorah Gisa bat Leib Yitzchak Halevi and Gittel. "May her soul be bound up in the bouquet of life."
- Lynnie Mirvis

*W*ith love to my very special granddaughter Shoshi in honor of her 24th birthday.
- Safta Sylvia

*W*ith gratitude to Hashem for the birth of our daughter Adina Rose Runya.
- The Tollivers

I honor the women in my family: my daughter Lilach; my daughters-in-law Tzipora & Mindy Sarah; my grandaughers Devora, Shayna, Shifra, Bracha, Mira, Becca, Navah, Emuna, Simcha & Ahuva.
- Gail Geula Winston

Approbations

בס"ד

Rabbi Eliezer Raphael (Lazer) Brody
**Author of Pi HaBe'er, Nafshi Tidom, The Trail to Tranquility, and
other books**
POB 11335
Ashdod, Israel 77112

16 Adar Bet, 5774

King Solomon, the wisest of all men, teaches: "Women's wisdom builds her
home" (Proverbs 14:1). Rabbenu Yona elaborates that a woman's special
capacity of insight is an integral part of her wisdom.

With Hashem's loving grace, my eyes have been rewarded the privilege of
seeing Rebbetzin Chana Bracha Siegelbaum's superb manuscript, *Ruth:
Gleaning the Fallen Sparks*, which so beautifully elaborates on the Book of
Ruth. As a woman of true valor and Director of the Midreshet B'erot Bat
Ayin, Rebbetzin Siegelbaum's inspiring and thoroughly enjoyable book
exemplifies a deep, comprehensible and refreshing insight on the Book of
Ruth. It not only grants special attention to its women-oriented aspects, but
gives the reader an exhilarating view of the subject from the angles of the
Oral Torah and Kabbalah as well.

Already an acclaimed and recognized expert and authority in the field of
Jewish women's education, Rebbetzin Siegelbaum's writings prove that she
is no less an expert with quill and parchment in hand. Her writings overflow
with emuna, the love of Torah and her fellow Jew, and the love of our holy
Land of Israel. This wonderful book should certainly grace the bookshelf of
every Jewish home.

May The Almighty help Rebbetzin Siegelbaum's wellsprings to flow forth,
and may she succeed in all her endeavors; seeing gratification from her
family and her students always while enjoying all the best of material and
spiritual blessings with long, healthy and happy years.

In eager anticipation of Moshiach, and the full redemption of our people and
the ingathering of the exiles in our beloved homeland of *Eretz Yisrael*,

Rabbi Eliezer Raphael (Lazer) Brody
Ashdod, Land of Israel

בן ציון רבינוביץ

בלאאמו"ר זצוקללה"ה

מביאלא

עיה"ק ירושלים תובב"א

בס"ד פעיה"ק ירושלים ת"ו יום ג' בשבת ט' אדר ב' תשע"ד

הובא לפני החיבור על מגילת רות בשם **רות - ליקוט הניצוצות הנפולים** הרואה אור ע"י מדרשת
בארות בת עין, המבאר בהרחבה את מעלת וסגולת הנשים וגיירי הצדק בדורינו, וכידוע שבתורה טמונים
סודות רבים ויש לפרש ולבאר אותם בלשון השווה לכל נפש שיוכלו להבין אותם כדבעי, ובפרט בדורנו
כשיש הרבה שאינם מבינים לשה"ק וצריך להסביר להם ולבאר להם באופן שיוכלו להבין את דברי התוה"ק.

וניכרת ההשקעה הגדולה בספר חשוב זה להסביר ולבאר את מגילת רות והוא מבוסס על מאמרי
חז"ל בדרך החסידות, ובוודאי יהי' לתועלת גדולה להמעיינים והלומדים בספר זה וזכות גדולה היא
להפיץ תורה ולהבין עמקות וסודות התורה, להוציא מליבם של האומרים שזה סיפור דברי היסטוריה
בעלמא ר"ל,

יעזור השי"ת שתזכו להרחבת הדעת ומנוחת הנפש וימלא השי"ת משאלות לבכם לטובה, ותוכלו
להמשיך ולהפיץ דבר ה' ולקרב יהודים לעבודתו יתברך שמו, וכימי מור והדם יראינו ה' נפלאות ונזכה
בקרוב לגאולה השלימה בביאת גואל צדק בב"א.

כ"ד המעתיר ומצפה להצלחתכם בכל הענינים לטובה ברו"ג

הכו"ח בדחשי ברכה והצלחה,

Approbations

בן ציון רבינוביץ
בלאאמו״ר זצוקללה״ה
מביאלא
עיה״ק ירושלים תובב״א

בס״ד

9 Adar Bet, 5774 Jerusalem, Israel

I was presented with the manuscript on *Megillat Ruth, Ruth: Gleaning the Fallen Sparks,* published by Midreshet B'erot Bat Ayin. It explains in great detail the merits of women and converts in our generation. As known, the Torah contains many concealed levels, and it is important to explain and clarify them in a language comprehensible to everyone. In our generation, when many Jews do not understand the Hebrew language, it is especially important to explain the words of the holy Torah in a way that everyone can understand.

The immense effort invested to explain and clarify *Megillat Ruth* is evident in this important book. The book is based on the teachings of our sages in the way of Chassidut. It is certainly extremely beneficial to learn and study this book in depth. It is a great merit to disseminate Torah and to understand the depths of the concealed matters of the Torah in order to refute those who claim that the Torah is a mere history book G-d forbid.

May Hashem grant you serenity and peace of mind. May He fulfill all your wishes for good, and may you be able to continue to publish words of Hashem, and bring Jews close to the service of G-d.

May Hashem show us wonders as in the days of Mordechai and Esther, and may we merit the complete redemption and the coming of our Righteous Redeemer, soon and in our days.

I sign with earnest hopes for your success in all matters, both spiritual and material, and with heartfelt blessings.

B.S.M. Ben Tzion Rabinowitz
of Biala

הכו״ח ברחשי ברכה והצלחה,

Table of Contents

Introduction

הקדמה

"*At* the time of Mashiach the lower will become higher and the hidden inner layer of reality will be revealed."[1] As we move forward in the Messianic age, we experience an increased interest in women's role of bringing about the final redemption.

Ruth, the mother of royalty, is the perfect role model and inspiration for women who aspire to follow her path of righteousness and make a difference in the world. She is particularly a role model for the many righteous converts who join the Jewish people at this time, before we reach the epoch when converts will no longer be accepted.[2]

The Scroll of Ruth takes place in the Land of Israel, during the bleak period of the Judges when there was a lack of unity and central leadership. This period parallels our current era, about which the following can also be ascribed: "In these days there is no king in Israel; each person does whatever is straight in his own eyes."[3]

In spite of, or perhaps because of, the fact that Ruth was a convert from the lowest people whose ability to convert was questionable, she nevertheless was able to shine her light amidst Israel's darkest times. Her light eventually brought about the sprout of Mashiach, through the birth of her great-grandson, King David.[4]

---

[1] Rabbi Yitzchak Ginsburgh, *Mashiach and Jewish Leadership*.
[2] *Babylonian Talmud, Avodah Zarah* 3b.
[3] *Shoftim* 17:6.
[4] *Megillat Ruth* 4:17.

Chapter One

From Ruth to David

מרות לדוד

$\mathcal{W}$ho wrote the Scroll of Ruth and why?
מי כתב את מגילת רות ולאיזו מטרה?

Shemuel the Prophet wrote *Megillat Ruth* to prove that not only is David a legitimate Jew, he, furthermore, descended from an extraordinary righteous convert.

> **...ומי כתבן משה כתב ספרו ופרשת בלעם ואיוב**
> **יהושע כתב ספרו ושמונה פסוקים שבתורה**
> **שמואל כתב ספרו ושופטים ורות כתב דוד כתב ספר**
> **תהלים...(תלמוד בבלי מסכת בבא בתרא יד/ב)**

...Who wrote [the books of the Tanach]? Moshe wrote his book and the sections about Bilam and Iyov. Yehoshua wrote his book and the [last] eight verses in the Torah. Shemuel wrote his book, the Book of *Shoftim* and *Ruth*. David wrote the Book of *Tehillim* (*Babylonian Talmud, Baba Batra* 14b).

Ruth–The Mother of Royalty   רות–אם המלכות

Although Ruth was a princess, the granddaughter of Eglon, the Moabite king,[5] she was considered to be from the lowest spiritual beginnings, since the Moabite people were one of the

---

5 *Babylonian Talmud, Nazir* 22b.

most despised nations. They apparently are barred from ever entering the Jewish congregation, as it states,

לֹא יָבֹא עַמּוֹנִי וּמוֹאָבִי בִּקְהַל הַשֵּׁם גַּם דּוֹר
עֲשִׂירִי לֹא יָבֹא לָהֶם בִּקְהַל הַשֵּׁם עַד עוֹלָם: עַל
דְּבַר אֲשֶׁר לֹא קִדְּמוּ אֶתְכֶם בַּלֶּחֶם וּבַמַּיִם בַּדֶּרֶךְ
בְּצֵאתְכֶם מִמִּצְרָיִם... (דברים כג:ד-ה)

"No Ammonite or a Moabite shall be admitted into the congregation of Hashem; none of their descendants, even in the tenth generation, shall ever be admitted into the congregation of Hashem, because they did not meet you with bread and water on the way, when you came out of Mitzrayim..." (*Devarim* 23:4-5).

Nevertheless, Ruth was able to elevate herself from her murky Moabite roots to become the great-grandmother of King David, from whom Mashiach will descend, speedily in our days! Ruth was willing to relinquish her own status of royalty for the sake of manifesting Hashem's royalty in the world. She left behind all of its wealth, comfort, security and honor for the sake of walking with Hashem and His people on the Jewish path of morality and kindness. In her desire and thirst to cleave to Hashem through Naomi, she was willing to exchange the honor of a princess for the disgrace of a lowly beggar, walking behind the Jewish farmers, gleaning fallen grains. Ruth was not even afraid to risk being an outcast who may never be accepted by the Jewish people, let alone ever finding a marriage partner among them.

...דאמר רבי יוחנן למה נקרא שמה רות שיצא
ממנה דוד שרייוהו להקב"ה בשירות ותושבחות:
(תלמוד בבלי מסכת בבא בתרא יד/ב)

Rabbi Yochanan asked, Why was her name Ruth? Because David, who satiated (*rivahu*) the Holy One, blessed be He, with hymns and praises, descended from her (*Babylonian Talmud, Baba Batra* 14b).

The Midrash teaches us that this essential quality, the quality of song, expressed through the melodies of *Tehillim* (Psalms), with its power to fluctuate from low to high and from high to low, enabled David, the composer of *Tehillim*, to emerge from Ruth. Perhaps Ruth's spiritual ascent from the lowest to the highest, together with sacrificing the highest physical comfort of a princess for the lowest status of a beggar, created a 'vibration' that generated the musical sequences of *Tehillim*, later composed by David. This diverse sequence is a vital quality for the King, enabling him to identify with, and include, the souls of all his people, from low to high, within him.

Her name, רות/Ruth, is derived from the root רְוָה/*rivah*, which means 'to satiate thirst.' The seed of Ruth's spiritual thirst to cleave to Hashem, regardless of the cost, later sprouted forth fruits by the way of David's *Tehillim*, satiating Hashem's thirst for the prayers of the righteous. When we are completely determined in our desire for spirituality and willing to pay the price, by overcoming the repeated obstacles that appear on the way, we, too, have the opportunity to perfect an attribute within us that can become manifested by our descendants and anchored in eternity.

Blemished Lineage?   יחוס פגום?

The Jewish people are a stiff-necked people.[6] One way this negative characteristic is expressed is through our tendencies to doubt the rabbinic authority to make halachic decisions. Even when a ruling has clearly been established and accepted by reputable halachic authorities, there will always be '*more pious than thou*' Jews who refuse to accept it. This is why there were those who regarded King David to be from a blemished lineage, since he was a descendant of Ruth, the Moabite convert.

---

[6] *Babylonian Talmud, Sanhedrin* 104b.

רבי אבא בר כהנא פתח (תהלים ד') רגזו
ואל תחטאו אמר דוד לפני הקב"ה עד
אימתי הם מתרגזים עלי ואומרים לא פסול
משפחה הוא ולא מרות המואביה הוא...
(מדרש רבה רות, ח:א)

Rabbi Abba, son of Kahana, opened by saying,
"Tremble, and sin no more..."[7] David said before G-d,
"Until when will they be agitated against me and say,
'Is he not from a blemished lineage? Is he not from
Ruth the Moabitess?'" (*Midrash Ruth Rabbah* 8:1).

King David's Jewish authenticity was challenged by skeptical
Jews. They insisted on emphasizing the literal meaning of the
Torah prohibition against accepting Moabite and Ammonite
converts. They consequently disregarded the rabbinic ruling
that clarifies this prohibition for the Moabite to "enter into
the congregation of Hashem" as applying only to the men,
but not to the women, "A Moabite but not a Moabitess," as
discussed in several places of the Talmud.[8] Boaz, the spiritual
leader of the generation,[9] instituted the ruling that allowed
Moabite women to convert because women were not expected
to go out and meet the Israelite travelers with bread and water,
since "the honor of the king's daughter is within."[10] This
ruling became accepted by the Sanhedrin of Boaz, and was
consequently handed over to the *Beit Din* (Jewish Court) of
Shemuel.

It is important to note that Boaz was totally impartial when
instituting this halachic ruling, as it took place prior to
his offering Ruth to a closer relative in levirate marriage.[11]
Nevertheless, David's Jewish lineage was questioned for several
generations afterwards, and he was held in disdain to such an

---

[7] *Tehillim* 4:5.
[8] *Babylonian Talmud, Yevamot* 69a, 76b, 77a; *Ketubot* 7b; *Kedushin* 75a.
[9] See Rashi, *Shoftim* 12:8, who identifies Ebtzan the Judge with Boaz.
[10] *Tehillim* 45:14.
[11] *Megillat Ruth* 4:5.

extent that Shemuel the Prophet felt compelled to write the Scroll of Ruth. This book proves that David was fit to be a King in Israel, as a legitimate Jew, descended from Ruth, the righteous convert.[12]

In addition to telling us about David's origin, *Megillat Ruth* also teaches us about the greatness of Ruth's selfless actions. The story of her life is related, not only for the sake of glorifying the genealogy of David; it furthermore has importance in its own right.[13] Through the exceptional *chesed* (loving-kindness) that Ruth showed her mother-in-law and her deceased husband, she rectified the lack of *chesed* that was inherent in the Moabite people from whom she descended.

[12] Rabbi Yehoshua Bachrach, *Mother of Royalty* (lecture at Michlalah – Jerusalem College for Women), quoting Rabbi Shlomo Alkabetz, *Shoresh Yishai,* in the name of Rabbi Shemaryah, *Commentary on the Five Megillot,* page 232.
[13] Rabbi Avraham Keriv, *Megillat Ruth.*

Chapter Two

Cleaving to the Land of Israel

להדבק בארץ ישראל

*T*he Consequences of Deserting the Land
ההשלכות של עזיבת הארץ

Megillat Ruth teaches us about the vital importance of living in the Land of Israel. The story of Elimelech's deserting the Land of Israel during a time of hardship had severe consequences for Elimelech and his family. In spite of the great qualities of this prominent Jewish family, they were stricken harshly for leaving the Land of Israel. Elimelech perished and his family became impoverished. After their camels and cattle had died, Elimelech's two sons also passed away.[14]

ת"ר אין יוצאין מארץ לחו"ל אא"כ עמדו
סאתים בסלע א"ר שמעון אימתי בזמן
שאינו מוצא ליקח אבל בזמן שמוצא ליקח
אפי' עמדה סאה בסלע לא יצא וכן היה
ר"ש בן יוחאי אומר אלימלך מחלון וכליון
גדולי הדור היו ופרנסי הדור היו ומפני מה
נענשו מפני שיצאו מארץ לחוצה לארץ...
(תלמוד בבלי מסכת בבא בתרא צא/א)

Our Rabbis taught, It is not permitted to leave the Land of Israel for a foreign country, unless two *se'ahs*[15] are sold for one *selah*.[16] Rabbi Shimon said, This is permitted only when one cannot find [anything] to

---

[14] Rashi, Rabbi Shlomo ben Yitzchak, (1040-1105), Troyes, France, a leading commentator on the Torah and the Talmud, *Megillat Ruth* 1:3.

[15] One *se'ah* equals approximately 8.3 liters (approximately 8.8 quarts).

[16] One *selah* equals 17 grams silver (0.60 oz).

buy, but when one is able to find something to buy, even if one *se'ah* costs a *selah*, one must not depart. And so said Rabbi Shimon bar Yochai, Elimelech, Machlon and Kiliyon were among the notables and leaders of their generation. Why, then, were they punished? Because they left *Eretz Yisrael* for a foreign country... (*Babylonian Talmud, Baba Batra* 91a; *Midrash Bereishit Rabbah* 28:3).

Yet, Elimelech and his family only left Israel to live temporaily (לָגוּר) outside of Israel. They didn't intend to settle and make themselves comfortable in one particular place, but only to wander around from place to place within the many fields of Moav (בִּשְׂדֵי מוֹאָב). Only afterwards did they gradually forget their original attachment to the Land of Israel.

וַיְהִי בִּימֵי שְׁפֹט הַשֹּׁפְטִים וַיְהִי רָעָב בָּאָרֶץ וַיֵּלֶךְ אִישׁ
מִבֵּית לֶחֶם יְהוּדָה **לָגוּר** בִּשְׂדֵי מוֹאָב הוּא וְאִשְׁתּוֹ
וּשְׁנֵי בָנָיו: וְשֵׁם הָאִישׁ אֱלִימֶלֶךְ וְשֵׁם אִשְׁתּוֹ נָעֳמִי
וְשֵׁם שְׁנֵי בָנָיו מַחְלוֹן וְכִלְיוֹן אֶפְרָתִים מִבֵּית לֶחֶם
יְהוּדָה **וַיָּבֹאוּ שְׂדֵי מוֹאָב וַיִּהְיוּ שָׁם**: וַיָּמָת אֱלִימֶלֶךְ
אִישׁ נָעֳמִי וַתִּשָּׁאֵר הִיא וּשְׁנֵי בָנֶיהָ: וַיִּשְׂאוּ לָהֶם
נָשִׁים מֹאֲבִיּוֹת שֵׁם הָאַחַת עָרְפָּה וְשֵׁם הַשֵּׁנִית רוּת
וַיֵּשְׁבוּ שָׁם כְּעֶשֶׂר שָׁנִים: (רות א:א-ד)

"It came to pass in the days when the judges judged, that there was a famine in the land. A certain man of Bethlehem in Judea went to sojourn in the fields of Moav: he, and his wife, and his two sons. The name of the man was Elimelech, and the name of his wife Naomi, and the names of his two sons were Machlon and Kiliyon, Ephrathites of Bethlehem in Judea. They came into the field of Moav, and they were there. Then Elimelech, Naomi's husband, died; and she was left with her two sons. They married Moabite women: one named Orpah and the other Ruth; and they settled there for about ten years" (*Megillat Ruth* 1:1-4).

Within the description of Elimelech's departure from the Land of Israel, there is a hidden praise to the rest of the Jewish people. In spite of the severe famine in the land, only one man left the Land of Israel; (וַיֵּלֶךְ אִישׁ),[17] and this man (Elimelech) only went to live temporarily (לָגוּר) outside of Israel. Yet, as often happens to Israelis who momentarily leave the Land of Israel, Elimelech got stuck. Although his intention was only to "sojourn temporarily" (לָגוּר) not even to settle in one specific field, but "sojourn in the fields of Moav," the *Megillah* notes that when he and his family came to the fields of Moav, "… they were there" (וַיִּהְיוּ שָׁם). That is to say, "they were [stuck] there," and began to see themselves as Moabites. Finally, after the death of Elimelech, his two sons married Moabite women and completely gave up on following through with their intentions to return to the Land of Israel. "They settled there" (וַיֵּשְׁבוּ שָׁם), the total of "about ten years" (כְּעֶשֶׂר שָׁנִים) a substantial time-period.[18]

What motivated Naomi and Ruth, her daughter-in-law, to return to the Land of Israel?

מה הניע את נעמי ורות כלתה לשוב לארץ ישראל?

וַיָּמוּתוּ גַם שְׁנֵיהֶם מַחְלוֹן וְכִלְיוֹן וַתִּשָּׁאֵר הָאִשָּׁה
מִשְּׁנֵי יְלָדֶיהָ וּמֵאִישָׁהּ: (רות א:ה)

"Both Machlon and Kiliyon died; so the woman was left without her two children and without her husband" (*Megillat Ruth* 1:5).

[17] Rabbi Moshe Alshich, (1508-1593), Turkey – Tzefat, halachic authority, inspiring teacher and Kabbalist, *Megillat Ruth* 1:1.
[18] Malbim, Rabbi Meir Loeb ben Yechiel Michael, (1809-1879), Volhynia, Ukraine, most prolific Torah exegete in modern time. Based upon accurate, linguistic rules, Malbim proves how the Oral Torah is necessary and implicit in the simple meaning of the verses and in the profundity of the language, *Megillat Ruth* 1:1-4.

When Naomi found herself left miserably alone with her two Moabite daughters-in-law, she discerned that her true place was in the Land of Israel. In spite of her desire to tend to the graves of her husband and sons, Naomi yearned more to return to the Land of the Living. She had aged beyond her years from the wretched agony of having lost her husband and two sons. However, this did not deter her from walking alone down the long, strenuous and dangerous road back to the Land of Hashem.

More than being ready for the difficult journey, Naomi was prepared to face the shame of exposing herself to her people as a broken woman, who had fallen from aristocracy and prominence. Nevertheless, the mere thought of returning to the Land of Israel invigorated her steps, while breathing new life into her swollen veins and wrinkled skin.

נפולה היתה, וקמה לה בחזירה לארץ ישראל:
(מדרש לקח טוב)

She was fallen, yet, she was now rising by returning to *Eretz Yisrael* (*Midrash Lekach Tov*).

Ruth, in turn, understood that the highest way to serve the G-d of Naomi and her people, was to return with her to the Land of the Jews. In her burning desire to embrace Judaism to its fullest in the Land of Israel, she was prepared to perform the greatest self-sacrifice. She not only risked living in poverty, but moreover, she was willing to become an outcast for the rest of her life, with no one to marry. Through Ruth's yearning to follow her mother-in-law to an unknown future in the Land of Israel, she surpassed the righteous convert, Yitro, who was unwilling to follow his son-in-law Moshe, but returned back to his fatherland.[19]

---

[19] *Bamidbar* 10:29-30.

Ruth, the Land of Israel and Mashiach
רות, ארץ ישראל והמשיח

The story of Ruth teaches us how the Land of Israel is the focal point of our Messianic vision. The Arizal[20] writes that Ruth's son, the grandfather of David, was called Oved, from the language of working, as he worked the Land of Israel.[21] Since bread is our ultimate 'hardworking food,' involving eleven steps of preparation (such as sowing, plowing, harvesting and winnowing) it represents the refinement of the human character that is necessary to bring the Mashiach.

Grain that is specifically grown in the Land of Israel is subject to the laws of the Land, as specified in the Torah: Leaving the corners for the poor and allowing them to glean and collect forgotten grain.[22] Following these agricultural laws, while reaping and harvesting grain, will eventually produce the bread of our refinement: Mashiach, the sprout of David, the perfect human being who reflects Hashem in all of his actions.

Mashiach, son of David, had to descend from a female immigrant, who was conscious of the agricultural cycle of the Land of Israel, and who developed a direct relationship with the land by gleaning its grain. Ruth's gleaning of grain in Beit-Lechem (House of Bread) was a vital part of an essential spiritual rectification process. The bread associated with the Mashiach from Beit-Lechem symbolizes this ultimate human refinement.

In this way, Ruth begins the process of our mutual efforts in reconnecting with the Land of Israel, which eventually brings about the Messianic fulfillment of peace and prosperity.

---

[20] Rabbi Yitzchak Luria Ashkenazi (Arizal), (1534-1572), Tzefat, leading Kabbalist, creator of Lurianic Kabbalah, the mystical interpretation of exile and redemption, through the process of *tikun* (rectification).
[21] Arizal, *Likutei Torah, Megillat Ruth.*
[22] *Vayikra* 19:9; *Devarim* 24:19.

Chapter Three

A Perfected Mother and Daughter-in-Law Relationship

יחס מושלם בין כלה לחמותה

$\mathcal{A}$ Challenging Relationship   יחס מאתגר

The relationship between mother-in-law and daughter-in-law is not simple, since there naturally is tension between women who become relatives when a son becomes a husband. These women may have an underlying tendency to compete for the devotion of the man who links them. It takes a certain spiritual maturity for a mother-in-law to accept the divine dictum: "…a man leaves his father and his mother and cleaves to his wife, and they become one flesh."[22] She must learn to accept that there is another woman who takes precedence in the life of her beloved son. On the other hand, it may be a challenge for the daughter-in-law to fulfill the command, "Honor your father and mother,"[23] toward the mother of her husband, the same way that she shows respect to her own mother.[24] The halacha presumes that there is biased antagonism between daughter-in-law and mother-in-law; therefore, they are prohibited from testifying against one another.

---

[22] *Bereishit* 2:24.

[23] *Shemot* 20:12.

[24] *Tur, Yore Deah* 240, *Shulchan Aruch, Yore Deah* 240:24, *Chaye Adam*, part 1, 67:24. Actually according to halacha, a married woman has a greater obligation to honor her in-laws than her own parents, since she is exempt from honoring her own parents due to her obligation to take care of her husband's needs (*Shulchan Aruch, Yore Deah* 240:17). Yet, she is still obligated to honor her own parents in any way that her husband allows (*Kitzur Shulchan Aruch* 143:13).

והכול נאמנים להעיד לה, עדות זו חוץ מחמש
נשים שחזקתן שונאות זו את זו, שאין מעידות
זו לזו במיתת בעלה, שמא יתכוונו לאוסרה
על בעלה, ועדיין הוא קיים; ואלו הן: חמותה,
ובת חמותה, וצרתה, ויבמתה, ובת בעלה:
(רמב"ם הלכות גירושין יב:טז)

Anyone may testify for a woman [that her husband
died], with the exception of the five women known to
be antagonistic toward each other. These women are:
the mother-in-law, the daughter of the mother-in-law,
the second wife, the sister-in-law and her husband's
daughter. These five are not permitted to testify for
each other regarding the death of a husband, lest they
intend to make her forbidden to her husband, [by
testifying that he has died] when he is actually still alive
[so that she will remarry on the basis of this testimony
and then become forbidden to her original husband]
(Rambam, *Mishna Torah, Laws of Divorce* 12:16).

Selfless Devotion to her Mother-in-Law
מסירות נפש לחמותה

In spite of this, Ruth, a daughter of Moav, was attached to
Naomi her mother-in-law and clung lovingly to her with the
words "Wherever you go I will go."[25] Naomi had imparted
to her daughters-in-law all the beautiful practices of the
Hebrew home, even in eating and drinking. Recognizing
the passionate devotion of a daughter-in-law toward the
mother of her departed husband allows us to appreciate the
high level of purity and warmth that permeated their family
life. Otherwise, we couldn't possibly comprehend the strong
ties that bound Ruth to this family. The strongest influence

---

[25] *Megillat Ruth* 1:16.

emanated from Naomi. She was refined in word and deed, and Ruth was drawn toward her like a planet gravitating toward the sun.[22]

Ruth was selflessly devoted to restoring the soul of her mother-in-law, both physically and spiritually. This Moabite princess lowered herself to become a beggar in Israel, in order to provide sustenance for her mother-in-law and preserve her honor. Ruth's *chesed* (kindness) toward Naomi was so extraordinary that it became the subject of amazement among the people of Beit-Lechem. Stories of her *chesed* even reached the ears of Boaz, the head of the Sanhedrin, (Jewish Court) who proclaimed, "It has been fully related to me, all that you have done to your mother-in-law after the death of your husband..."[23] Malbim notes that Ruth's *chesed* was completely beyond nature; since her husband had died, it could not be said that Ruth's kindness toward her mother-in-law was in order to please her husband.

Ruth lived her entire life for the sake of Naomi, who was foremost in her thoughts, and with whom she shared every gift and accomplishment. When Boaz offered her a meager meal, it was inconceivable for Ruth to partake of it without putting some of it aside for Naomi.[24] As soon as Ruth had completed the gleaning, "...she returned to her mother-in-law."[25] Though she cleaved to Boaz's young women for a lengthy period of time, it only lasted as long as she had to glean, as it states, "She cleaved to Boaz's maidservants to glean..."[26] However, afterwards when there was nothing left to glean, she immediately returned to her mother-in-law and did not visit Boaz's maidens, for the love for her mother-in-law was stronger than anything else in her heart.

---

[22] Nachal Yosef, *Megillat Ruth*.
[23] *Megillat Ruth*. 2:11.
[24] Ibid. 2:18.
[25] Ibid. 23.
[26] Ibid.

Ruth offered Naomi the best from everything she received. She happily shared with her mother-in-law Boaz's engagement gift of six grains, putting Boaz's own words in her mouth, "For he said to me, 'Do not go empty-handed to your mother-in-law.'"[27] This statement, understood both on a literal and metaphorical level, became Ruth's *raison d'etre*. It was even said of her own child that she bore, "A son is born to Naomi."[28]

Sensitive Reproach to her Daugher-in-Law
תוכחה רגישה לכלתה

Naomi, in turn, related to Ruth as a loving mother would treat her own child and called her "my daughter" throughout the Megillah.[29] Naomi knew how to guide Ruth in a kind and caring manner, as a teacher and mentor, without acting like a critical mother-in-law. Although Ruth had long converted to Judaism, Scripture still calls her "The Moabitess,"[30] because she spoke like one when she misquoted Boaz. She said, "Also, he said unto me: 'You shall cleave to **my young men**,'"[31] when in truth, he told her to cleave to his **young women**.[32] Apparently, a residue of the Moabite way still clung to Ruth's vocabulary.

ותאמר רות המואביה אל נעמי, אמר ר'
יוחנן ודאי מואביה היא שהוציאה עילה
על אותו צדיק, הוא אמר לה וכה תדבקין
עם נערותי והיא אומרת לחמותה עם
הנערים אשר לי תדבקין, ואף נעמי אמרה
ברוח הקדש טוב בתי כי תצאי עם נערותיו:
(ילקות שמעוני רות, ג:תרד)

---

27 Ibid. 3:17.
28 Ibid. 4:17.
29 Altogether seven times: *Megillat Ruth* 1:11, 1:12, 2:2, 2:22, 3:1, 3:16, 3:18.
30 Ibid. 2:21.
31 Ibid.
32 Ibid. 8.

Rabbi Yochanan said, She was indeed a Moabitess, to utter such slander against that righteous man. He said to her, "Cleave to my maidens." And she said to her mother-in-law: "You shall cleave to my young men." However, Naomi said in *Ruach Hakodesh* (divine inspiration), "It is good my daughter that you go out with his maidservants" (*Yalkut Shimoni Ruth* 3:604).

Naomi neither ignored Ruth's slip, in fear of offending her daughter-in-law, nor did she make Ruth lose face by confronting her directly regarding her mistake. Rather, she gently set her on the right course, with an endearing demeanor and with loving words, "It is good my daughter, that you go out with his maidservants...[33] We can just imagine Naomi's loving voice as she calls her "my daughter," putting her arm around Ruth, while indirectly correcting her remark and fine-tuning Ruth's vocabulary.

Benefitting her Daughter-in-Law   הטבה לכלתה

When rays of hope were reawakened in Naomi for the restoration of her deceased son's soul through the mitzvah of *yibum* (Levirate Marriage),[34] Naomi's foremost thought was how to benefit Ruth. "My daughter, I will seek for you rest which will be **good for you**."[35] With these words Naomi recognized Ruth's need for a husband, since there is no rest for a woman until she marries.[36] As it states, "May you find rest each of you in the house of her husband."[37] Yet marriage, in

---

[33] *Megillat Ruth* 2:22.
[34] See chapter 8 of this book for a thorough explanation of *yibum*.
[35] *Megillat Ruth* 3:1.
[36] Rabbi Avraham Ibn Ezra, (1089-1164), Tudela, Spain, one of the most distinguished Jewish scholars and writers of the Middle Ages, *Megillat Ruth* 3:1.
[37] *Megillat Ruth* 1:9.

itself, was not all that Naomi wished for Ruth. Only a marriage to a man who keeps Torah and mitzvot, "will be good for you."[38] Boaz was not only the perfect candidate to restore the lost soul of Naomi's son Machlon, as the head of the Sanhedrin,[39] and the greatest Torah scholar of the generation, he moreover would be the very best husband she could wish for Ruth.

Yet, Naomi intuitively understood that although Boaz was wealthy and the leader of the generation, he was humble and felt unworthy of the beautiful Ruth who was half his age.[40] Boaz would not take advantage of his position to make Ruth an offer that she would be uncomfortable refusing. Although he was aware of the importance of the mitzvah of *yibum*, Boaz would not want to impose on Ruth, unless she was likeminded in her intend to fulfill this mitzvah. He needed a sign from Ruth. Therefore, Naomi knew that the only way for Boaz to propose to Ruth was if Ruth went down to the threshing floor in her finery to lie at his feet. From the spelling, our Rabbis sensed Naomi's trepidation at sending Ruth off on such a mission. She sympathized with Ruth, who might not have had the temerity for this, or who otherwise would have doubted the propriety of such an act. Naomi, therefore, assigned herself to the deed, as she told Ruth, "you shall go down (וְיָרַדְתְּ). The word is actually written with a *yud* indicating, "I shall go down" (וְיָרַדְתִּי)[41] (to connect my soul with yours, through this mitzvah, in a way that you will connect with me in the future). Similarly, when Rivkah sent Ya'acov to deceive Yitzchak, she said, "Upon me be your curse, my son."[42]

Ruth responded, "Whatever you will say **to me** I will do."[43] The word אֵלַי/*elai* ("to me") is read, but not transcribed in the text. Only the vowels are written to convey that although the

---

[38] Malbim, *Megillat Ruth* 3:1.

[39] Rabbi Moshe Alshich, *Megillat Ruth* 4:1.

[40] Ruth was forty years old while Boaz was eighty (*Midrash Ruth Rabbah* 6:2).

[41] *Megillat Ruth* 3:3.

[42] *Bereishit* 27:13; Rabbi Yehoshua Bachrach, *Mother of Royalty*, page 107.

[43] *Megillat Ruth* 3:4.

advice seemed improper to Ruth, she nevertheless would not do otherwise, since Naomi had given it,[44] as if to say, "I do not intend for myself (אֵלַי)(for my own benefit), but only in order to establish your words." The word אֵלַי is missing because Ruth had effaced herself completely before her mother-in-law, who had issued the command.[45]

Despite Ruth's self-effacement and obedience to Naomi, she nevertheless did not lose her individuality and personal common sense. A close reading and comparison between *Megillat Ruth* 3:3 and 3:6 reveals a difference between Naomi's command, and the way in which Ruth fulfilled it.

ותרד הגורן ותעש-היא אמרה לה ורחצת וסכת
ושמת שמלותיך עליך ואחר כך וירדת הגורן
והיא לא עשתה כן אלא אמרה אם ארד כשאני
מקושטת הפוגע בי והרואה אותי יאמר שאני
זונה לפיכך ירדה בתחילה הגורן. ואחר כך קשטה
את עצמה כאשר צותה חמותה: (רש"י, רות ג:ו)

GO DOWN TO THE THRESHINGFLOOR AND DO – She [Naomi] told her to wash, anoint and get dressed up, then afterwards to go down to the threshing floor. She [Ruth] did not do this but said, "If I go down all dressed up, anyone who sees me will think that I am a prostitute." Therefore, she first went down to the threshing floor, and only afterwards did she get dressed up the way her mother-in-law had commanded (*Rashi, Megillat Ruth* 3:6).

Ruth had learned from Naomi to become in tune with true *tzniut* (modesty in dress and behavior). She learned an even higher degree of *tzniut*, by taking the loving reproach of her mother-in-law and teacher a step further!

---

[44] Rabbi Yitzchak Arama, *Akeidat Yitzchak,* quoted by Rabbi Yehoshua Bachrach, *Mother of Royalty,* page 108.
[45] Rabbi Yehoshua Bachrach, *Mother of Royalty,* page 108.

Who are you my Daughter?   מי את בתי?

Upon Ruth's return the next morning, Naomi carefully avoided being a prying mother-in-law by restraining herself from showering her daughter-in-law with boundless questions. During Ruth's potentially fatal mission at Boaz's feet, Naomi had remained awake all night. Her heart trembled expectantly. If only she could pour out all of the thoughts and feelings in her heart with all the questions she wanted to ask... Yet, when Ruth returned in the morning, Naomi asked her only one short and modest question, phrased with utmost care and with true motherly wisdom, "Who are you, my daughter?"[46] Are you still Ruth the Moabitess or have you become Mrs. Boaz?

---

[46] *Megillat Ruth* 3:16, Rabbi Yehoshua Bachrach, *Mother of Royalty*, page 120.

Chapter Four

Righteous Convert

גיורת צדק

The meaning of the name Ruth

משמעות השם רות

One of the reasons we read *Megillat Ruth* on Shavuot is because not only is Ruth the archetype of a righteous convert, but the entire Jewish people were also 'converts' when we received the Torah on Shavuot. The name Ruth alludes to her conversion, as its numerical value equals 606. This is the number of mitzvot that Ruth, the righteous gentile, accepted upon herself when she joined the Jewish people. The Seven Noachide Laws that she had kept all along, together with the numerical value of her name, add up to the 613 mitzvot of the Torah.[48]

The name Ruth is related to the word רְוָיָה/*revaya*, which denotes satisfying the spiritual thirst[49] that Ruth expressed in her desire to follow Naomi, and become part of her people. Rabbi Hirsch[50] relates her name to the Hebrew word רְעוּת/ *reut*, which means 'friend' or 'connected.' Ruth yearned to be connected with the people of Israel, and she was finally accepted. Ruth's desire to convert is contrasted with Orpah's kissing her mother-in-law goodbye, by the following words, "Orpah kissed her mother-in-law, but Ruth cleaved to her"

---

[48] The *Shelah HaKadosh*, Rabbi Yesha'ya Horowitz, (1565-1630), Prague–Tzefat, halachist and Kabbalist, who influenced the Ba'al Shem Tov greatly, *Haghot l'mesechet Shavuot*.

[49] See this book, chapter 1. ***From Ruth to David***, *Mother of Royalty*.

[50] Rabbi Shimshon Raphael Hirsch, (1808-1888), Hamburg, Germany, Chief Rabbi of Moravia and Austrian Silesia, founder of *Torah im Derech Eretz*– (The Integration of Torah with Worldly Involvement).

(וְרוּת דָּבְקָה בָּהּ).[51] The Hebrew word בָּהּ can either mean "to her" (to Naomi) or "to the letter *heh*" which represents Hashem. Ruth was indeed cleaving to Hashem through Naomi. So strong was Ruth's devotion to G-d, as well as to Judaism, that she clung to Naomi who represented both to her.

It is also possible to explain that Ruth was cleaving to מַלְכוּת/ *malchut*,[52] represented by the letter *heh*. According to Kabbalah, each of the main characters of *Megillat Ruth* corresponds to one of the letters of Hashem's four lettered name. Elimelech corresponds to *yud* (חָכְמָה/*chachma*—wisdom), Naomi to the first *heh* (בִּינָה/*bina*—understanding), Machlon, Ruth's first husband to the *vav* (the six middle *sefirot*) and Ruth to the last *heh* of Hashem's name (מַלְכוּת/*malchut*—royalty).[53]

The name רוּת/Ruth, if reversed, spells out תּוֹר/ *Tor*, the Hebrew word for dove, to which the Jewish People is compared.[54] By adding the letter *heh* to *Tor* you get the word תּוֹרָה/Torah. Ruth accepted the entire Torah when she decided to follow her mother-in-law to the Land of Israel. This is in spite of the gloomy prospects for building her future there, since it hadn't yet been clarified that a Moabite woman would be accepted as a convert to the Jewish people.

רות הפכה לשמה וכו, רות, שהיא ה' אחרונה, מלכות, הפכה את שמה רות, אל תור. שנאמר, ותור וגוזל. כי מלכות נקראת ג"כ תור. וכן כתוב, יונתי בחגוי הסלע בסתר המדריגה הראיני את מראיך השמיעיני את קולך כי קולך ערב ומראך נאוה. הרי שהמלכות נקראת יונה דהיינו תור: (זהר חדש, מדרש רות ו)

[51] *Megillat Ruth* 1:14.
[52] The revelation of G-d's kingdom, the last of G-d's Ten Manifestations (*sefirot*). A *sefirah* (pl. *sefirot*) is a channel of divine energy or life-force that emanates from G-d's infinite light to create what we experience as finite reality. These channels are called the Ten *Sefirot*—Ten Divine Emanations. The *sefirot* are also reflected in the human psyche representing the characteristics which G-d inserted into the world.
[53] *Tikunei Zohar* 75b; Arizal, *Likutei Torah, Megillat Ruth*.
[54] See Rashi, *Bereishit* 15:10.

RUTH REVERSED HER NAME ETC. Ruth, which is the last *heh* referring to 'kingdom,' reversed her name Ruth to *Tor*, as it states, "A turtledove *(tor)* and a young pigeon,"[55] for kingdom is also called a 'dove' *(tor)*. Thus it states, "O my dove, who are in the clefts of the rock, in the secret places of the cliff, let me see your countenance. Let me hear your voice, for your voice is sweet and your countenance is comely."[56] Behold, kingdom is called 'pigeon,' meaning 'dove' (*Zohar Chadash, Midrash Ruth* 6).

The *Zohar* makes a direct link between the name רות/Ruth when reversed to תור/*Tor* (dove) and the Davidic Kingdom which originated from her. The dove is associated with 'kingdom' because the king rules his people through the power of his speech (voice), and the dove is a singing bird whose voice we desire to hear. We may venture to say that it was Ruth's spiritual thirst that enabled her to birth a spark into the world that would someday become the quintessential song expressed in David's *Tehillim*. The songs of David that were sung in the Temple are intrinsically related to David's ability to establish Hashem's Kingdom on Earth.

Turning Ruth Away   דחיית רות

The process of Ruth's conversion was, indeed, far from smooth. Actually, we learn from the story of Ruth that one must discourage a conversion candidate, as Naomi turned Ruth away three times.[57] The Midrash learns the law about turning away a convert three times, from the three times Naomi mentioned the word "return."

Bereishit 15:9.
Shir HaShirim 2:14.
See *Megillat Ruth* 1:8-9, 1:11-13, 1:15.

לכנה שובנה. רבי שמואל בר חייא בש"ר חנינא
בשלשה מקומות כתיב כאן שובנה, שלשה
פעמים שובנה כנגד שלשה ימים שדוחים את
הגר, אם הטריח יותר מדאי מקבלים אותו,
א"ר יצחק בחוץ לא ילין גר דלתי לאורח
אפתח, לעולם תהא דוחה בשמאול ומקרב
בימין: (ילקוט שמעוני רות, א:תרא)

GO RETURN – Rabbi Shemuel Bar Chiya said in
the name of Rabbi Chanina, "Return" is written three
times here, corresponding to the three times one must
push away a convert. If he persists we accept him. Rabbi
Yitzchak says, "But the stranger shall not lodge in the
street, I will open my doors to the traveler."[58] One must
always push away with the left [hand] and bring close
with the right [hand] (*Yalkut Shimoni Ruth* 1:601).

Naomi actually kept this balance of pushing away and bringing
close through the phrase "go, return," with which she related to her
Moabite daughters-in-law. With the word "go" she pushed them
away; yet, simultaneously, with the word "return" she hinted at the
possibility of returning to Israel with her.[59] All of Naomi's words were
to test the sincerity of her daughters-in-law's intentions to convert.

"RETURN MY DAUGHTERS to Hashem through
me, AND GO afterwards to your land, and there you
will return and serve G-d." She spoke thus in order
that her right hand might bring close without pushing
them away with both hands. Naomi knew that if they
went back, they would serve the gods of their homelands
(Rabbi Moshe Alshich, *Megillat Ruth*, chapter 1).

For Orpah, Naomi's arguments were enough to weaken her
determination to return with Naomi. She kissed her mother-
in-law goodbye to return to her people and to her god.[60]

---

[58] *Iyov* 31:32.
[59] Rabbi Moshe Alshich, *Megillat Ruth* 1:8.
[60] *Megillat Ruth* 1:14.

Ruth's Declaration of Faith

הצהרת האמונה של רות

וַתֹּאמֶר רוּת אַל תִּפְגְּעִי בִי לְעָזְבֵךְ לָשׁוּב מֵאַחֲרָיִךְ
כִּי אֶל אֲשֶׁר תֵּלְכִי אֵלֵךְ וּבַאֲשֶׁר תָּלִינִי אָלִין עַמֵּךְ
עַמִּי וֵאלֹהַיִךְ אֱלֹהָי: בַּאֲשֶׁר תָּמוּתִי אָמוּת וְשָׁם
אֶקָּבֵר... (רות א:טז - יז)

"But Ruth replied, 'Do not entreat me to leave you,
to turn back and not follow you. For wherever you
go, I will go; wherever you lodge, I will lodge, your
people are my people; and your G-d is my G-d.
Wherever you die, I will die, and there I will be
buried...'" (*Megillat Ruth* 1:16-17).

Ruth resisted Naomi's dissuasion by pouring forth her love
and utter devotion with words that were akin to a powerful
and passionate melody. She opened her declaration of faith
with the words אַל תִּפְגְּעִי בִי which are usually translated
as, "Do not entreat me," however, the Hebrew word תִּפְגְּעִי
from the root פגע has several meanings. The most common
meaning is "to kill."[61] Ruth was telling Naomi, "Do not kill
me!" "Leaving me behind would be like killing me."[62]   Her
devotion to become Jewish was so strong that she would have
felt spiritually dead otherwise. Alternatively, the phrase אַל
תִּפְגְּעִי בִי can mean, "Don't get punished because of me."
Ruth was telling Naomi, "Do not sin on account of separating
from me. Since I am determined to go to Israel and become
Jewish, in any case, it is better to convert through you and not
through someone else. Do not assault me; your offence is not
justified in me as in Orpah, for a different spirit is within me,
to follow G-d."[63]

---

[61] See for example I *Shemuel* 22:17, I *Melachim* 2:25.
[62] Malbim, *Megillat Ruth* 1:16.
[63] *Midrash Ruth Rabbah* 2:23.

The word לְעָזְבֵךְ –"to leave you" and the phrase לָשׁוּב מֵאַחֲרָיִךְ –"to turn back and not follow you" seem redundant. Ruth was emphasizing, "All your prodding to make me return to my people could never make me leave G-d; it could only make me turn away from FOLLOWING AFTER YOU. I request to go WHEREVER YOU GO. I am going toward the same goal as you. Just as your purpose of going is in order to keep the Torah and mitzvot of the Land of Israel, so is my purpose of going. I am not seeking external success, or to meet a rich man to marry. Rather, WHEREVER YOU LODGE, I WILL LODGE. I realize that this world is only a temporary dwelling place, my ultimate destination is to keep the customs of the Jewish people and the Torah of Hashem. Because of my fervent belief, YOUR PEOPLE ARE already MY PEOPLE and so is YOUR G-D. WHEREVER YOU DIE, I WILL DIE. "I desire to die in the Land of Israel, with the righteous Jewish people, together with you, so our spirit will return to the bundle of eternal life. AND THERE I WILL BE BURIED –I am determined to be buried in the same place as you, in the Holy Land, among the graves of the righteous, who are ready to arise during the revival of the dead."[64]

Ruth concludes her declaration of faith by an antecedent to-the-grave-vow 'till death do us part.' Her life-and-death attachment to Naomi rectified the separation of her forefather Lot from Avraham, which led him to leave Avraham's path of righeousness. Ruth restored Lot's original closeness to Avraham, by returning to the place from which Lot departed. Scripture alludes to this rectification; coming full-circle by using the same word to describe both Lot's separation from Avraham, and Ruth's (a descendant of Lot) attachment to Naomi (a descendant of Avraham).

כֹּה יַעֲשֶׂה הַשֵׁם לִי וְכֹה יֹסִיף כִּי הַמָּוֶת יַפְרִיד... בֵּינִי וּבֵינֵךְ: (רות א:יז)

---

[64] Malbim, *Megillat Ruth* 1:16-17, based on *Midrash Ruth Rabbah* 2:23.

"...Thus and more may Hashem do to me, if anything but **death separate you from me**" (*Megillat Ruth* 1:17).

וַיֹּאמֶר אַבְרָם אֶל לוֹט אַל נָא תְהִי מְרִיבָה בֵּינִי וּבֵינֶךָ וּבֵין רֹעַי וּבֵין רֹעֶיךָ כִּי אֲנָשִׁים אַחִים אֲנָחְנוּ: הֲלֹא כָל הָאָרֶץ לְפָנֶיךָ **הִפָּרֶד נָא** מֵעָלַי אִם הַשְּׂמֹאל וְאֵימִנָה וְאִם הַיָּמִין וְאַשְׂמְאִילָה: (בראשית יג:ח - ט)

"Avram said to Lot, 'Let there be no strife please between me and you, between my herdsmen and your herdsmen; for we are brothers. Is not the whole land before you? **Separate yourself,** please, from me. If you go left I will go right, and if you go right I will go left'" (*Bereishit* 13:8-9).

The Midrash turns Ruth's monologue into a dialogue, and reveals from between the lines the teachings of Naomi, to which Ruth responded with each of her expressions of faith. Rashi comments in a similar vein with a different twist.

...מכל מקום דעתי להתגייר אלא מוטב על ידך ולא ע"י אחרת כיון ששמעה נעמי כך התחילה סודרת לה הלכות גרים אמרה לה בתי אין דרכן של בנות ישראל לילך לבתי תיאטראות ולבתי קרקסיאות שלהם אמרה לה אל אשר תלכי אלך אמרה לה בתי אין דרכן של ישראל לדור בבית שאין שם מזוזה אמרה לה באשר תליני אלין עמך עמי אלו עונשין ואזהרות ואלהיך אלהי שאר מצוות: (מדרש רבה רות, ב:כב)

"...In any case, I am fully resolved to convert, but it is better that it should be at your hands than at those of another." When Naomi heard this, she began to unfold to her the laws of conversion. She said to her, "My daughter, it is not the way of the daughters of Israel to go to the theater houses and circuses." Ruth answered, "WHEREVER YOU GO I WILL GO." Naomi said to her, "My daughter, it is not the way of a Jew to live in a house without a mezuzah." Ruth answered her, "WHEREVER YOU LODGE I WILL LODGE." "YOUR PEOPLE SHALL BE MY PEOPLE" [expresses her willingness to accept] the punishments and warnings, and "YOUR G-D IS MY G-D" [expresses her willingness to accept] the rest of the mitzvot (*Midrash Ruth Rabbah* 2:22).

אל תפגע בי - אל תפצרי בי. כי אל אשר
תלכי אלך - מכאן אמרו רבותינו ז"ל גר שבא
להתגייר מודיעים לו מקצת עונשים שאם בא
לחזור בו יחזור שמתוך דברים של רות אתה
למד שאמרה לה נעמי אסור לנו לצאת חוץ
לתחום בשבת א"ל באשר תלכי אלך, אסור לנו
להתייחד נקבה עם זכר שאינה אישה אמרה
לה באשר תליני אלין, עמנו מובדלים משאר
עמים בשש מאות ושלש עשרה מצוות עמך
עמי, אסור לנו ע"א אלהיך אלהי, ארבע מיתות
נמסרו לבית דין באשר תמותי אמות, שני
קברים נמסרו לבית דין אחד לנסקלין ונשרפין
ואחד לנהרגין ונחנקין אמרה לה ושם אקבר:
(רש"י, רות א:טז)

DO NOT ENTREAT ME – Do not implore me. "FOR WHEREVER YOU GO I WILL GO." From here our rabbis learned that when someone wants to convert, one must inform him of the punishments so that he will [become Jewish with complete knowledge of this]. From Ruth's words you learn that Naomi told her, "It is forbidden for us to go out of the Shabbat bounds." Ruth answered, "WHEREVER YOU GO I WILL GO." "It is forbidden for a female to be alone with a male who is not her husband" [to which she

answered], "WHEREVER YOU LODGE I WILL
LODGE." [Naomi said], "Our people is separated
from other people with 613 mitzvot." [Ruth answered],
"YOUR PEOPLE SHALL BE MY PEOPLE." "Idol
worship is forbidden for us" – "YOUR G-D IS MY
G-D." "Four kinds of death penalties were handed
over to the Jewish court." "WHEREVER YOU DID,
I WILL DIE." "Two kinds of graves were handed over
to the Jewish court, one for those stoned and burned
and another for those killed and strangled. [Ruth
answered], "THERE I WILL BE BURIED" (Rashi,
Megillat Ruth 1:16).

It is interesting to note how Rashi complements the Midrash
by reverting the negative into positive mitzvot. While the
Midrash has Naomi warn Ruth about going to the immodest
theater-houses and circuses; the equivalents of today's
discothèques. According to Rashi, Naomi taught Ruth about
the boundaries of Shabbat. One of the first steps a convert or a
ba'al teshuva[65] takes on her journey is to cut out inappropriate
social interaction and entertainment, and replace it with
Shabbat observance.

The mezuzah characterizes a Jewish home, and the *Shema*
(declaring the unity of Hashem) is written within it. According
to Rashi, Naomi took this notion a step further when she
taught Ruth about the Jewish way of expressing Hashem's unity
in the way we relate to others within the walls of our homes.
According to the Laws of *yichud* (seclusion), one is only allowed
to be alone with a person of the opposite sex with whom the
relationship has been sanctified by the unity of Hashem.

Rashi emphasizes that more than warning Ruth against the
punishment for not keeping the mitzvot, Naomi was teaching
Ruth the binding authority of the 613 mitzvot of the Torah.

---

[65] Newcomer to authentic Judaism, literally 'Master of Return.'

In addition, Rashi explains that Naomi singled out the prohibition of idol-worship, since this reflects a fundamental difference between Ruth's background and the Torah. Only Rashi interprets the last two parts of Ruth's declaration of faith as an indication that Naomi had more warnings for Ruth. Perhaps Naomi reminded Ruth that a *beit din* would be able to execute her for those transgressions that she would have been perfectly free to do, prior to conversion.

Alshich retains Ruth's declaration of faith as a monologue. He perceives Ruth's soul speaking through her words, and proclaiming her eternal truth. When Ruth's soul declared, "Wherever you go, I go," she referred to the final purpose and eternal resting place where all souls eventually must arrive. "Wherever you lodge, I will lodge," refers to the soul of the convert, attaching herself to a righteous Jew, and becoming her outer manifestation, like a garment. "Your people are my people," continues to describe the journey of the soul; when she reaches her ultimate resting place, she will be joined with the soul of her people. "Your G-d is my G-d," refers to how Hashem joins His name to a righteous person after his death.[66] Ruth's soul proclaimed that she would die and be buried in the same place as Naomi, since the entry to the Garden of Eden is in the Land of Israel from where the resurrection begins.

Being buried outside of the Land is like being held by a step-mother, whereas being buried inside the Land of Israel is like being cradled in the mother's arms.

---

[66] See Rashi, *Bereishit* 28:13.

Megillat Ruth 1:16-17	*Midrash Rabbah*	Rashi	Alshich
אֶל אֲשֶׁר תֵּלְכִי אֵלֵךְ *Wherever you go, I will go;*	Don't go to the theater houses and circuses.	*Techum Shabbat* Keep the boundary of Shabbat.	A person goes toward his or her eternal resting place.
וּבַאֲשֶׁר תָּלִינִי אָלִין *And wherever you lodge, I will lodge,*	Don't live in a house without a mezuzah.	*Yichud*-Seclusion Keep the laws pertaining to a man and a woman being alone together.	The soul of the convert becomes a garment for the righteous.
עַמֵּךְ עַמִּי *Your people are my people;*	Punishments and warnings	Israel is distinguished with 613 mitzvot.	The souls of the family welcome the deceased.
וֵאלֹהַיִךְ אֱלֹהָי *and your G-d is my G-d.*	Acceptance of the rest of the mitzvot	Prohibition of idol-worship.	G-d joins His name to the *tzaddik* after his death.
בַּאֲשֶׁר תָּמוּתִי אָמוּת *Wherever you die, I will die,*		Four kinds of death penalties.	It is best for the soul when the body is buried in the Land of Israel.
וְשָׁם אֶקָּבֵר *And there I will be buried.*		Two kinds of graves.	

Ruth & Orpah

רות וערפה

אמר רבי יוחנן צריך אדם לחוש לשם,
מחלון שהוא לשון מחילה, נזדווגה לו רות
שהיתה מרתתת מן העבירות, כליון כליה,
נזדווגה לו ערפה שיצאת ממנה גלית...
(ילקוט שמעוני רות, א:תר)

Rabbi Yochanan said, "A person needs to take note that the name Machlon is the language of *mechila* [forgiveness]. He married Ruth who shuddered at the thought of sin. Kiliyon is the language of *keliyah* [destruction]. He married Orpah from whom Goliat descended..." (*Yalkut Shimoni Ruth* 1:600).

Ruth teaches us that our deeds have consequences; not only for the outcome of our own life, but for future generations as well. Especially when being so close to *kedusha* (holiness), taking just one step in the wrong direction has serious consequences. When a person rejects the opportunity offered for rectification, this opportunity may never present itself again. Moreover, by not choosing 'life' at a given moment, one by default chooses 'death' and spiritual decline.

This is why the worst impurity clung to Orpah after she turned her back to Naomi. Our rabbis taught that on her way back to Moav she was violated by one hundred men and a dog. The difference between Ruth and Orpah teaches us how vitally important it is to seize opportunities for spiritual growth, whenever they present themselves. There is no status quo in the Torah, as it states, "The way of life above is to the wise, in order that he might avoid descending to the pit below."[67]

כתיב ממערות פלשתים וקרי ממערכות מלמד
שהערו באמו שבאו עליה מאה אנשים בלילה
אחת וכלב שנאמר. (שם מג) הכלב אנכי: (בתי
מדרשות, חלק ב, מדרש חסרות ויתרות שמואל א)

---

[67] *Mishlei* 15:24.

It states, "Out of the caves (מִמַּעֲרוֹת) of the P'lishtim," but
it reads, "Out of the ranks (מִמַּעֲרְכוֹת) of the P'lishtim."[68]
This teaches that they noted about his mother that one
hundred Pelishtim and a dog came upon her in one
night, as it states, (I *Shemuel* 17:23) "Am I a dog..."
(*Batei Midrashot*, part 2, *Midrash I Shemuel*).

In order to avoid sinking into impurity, we must always look
for spiritual growth and attach ourselves to people who bring
us closer to Hashem. A crucial decision, made at a turning
point in our lives, can have a striking impact on the lives of our
descendants. As according to the Midrash, one step in opposite
directions determined the difference between David and Goliat.

Ruth & Yitro   רות ויתרו

Ruth is only one of many righteous converts in the Torah.
Rachav, Bitya and Yitro are other examples of converts
mentioned in the Tanach. The name יִתְרוֹ/Yitro has the same
letters as Ruth with an added letter *yud;* actually it can be
unscrambled to spell her possible nickname, רוּתִי/Ruthi.
Although *yud* is the letter of wisdom, of which Yitro had much,
Ruth surpassed Yitro in her desire to live in Israel. Yitro, on the
other hand, refused to follow the Jewish people to the Land of
Israel, as he expressed, "I will not go, but I will depart to my
own land, and to my kindred."[69] This contrast is emphasized by
the comforting words of Boaz, "May Hashem recompense your
deed, and may a full reward be given you by Hashem, the G-d
of Israel, under whose wings you have come to take refuge."[70]
Rabbi Chasa emphasizes, "You have come."[71]

---

[68] I *Shemuel* 17:23.
[69] *Bamidbar* 10:30.
[70] *Megillat Ruth* 2:12.
[71] *Midrash Ruth Rabbah* 5:4.

The great reward that Ruth received was the result not only of her sincere conversion, but also of her deep understanding and conviction to come to the Land of Israel and join the Jewish people there. This is how Ruth surpassed Yitro in greatness.

Precious Convert   גיורת יקרה

The Torah emphasizes the mitzvah to be kind to the convert numerous times. For example, "You shall not oppress a convert; for you know the heart of a convert, seeing you were strangers in the land of Egypt."[72] "You shall love the convert; for you were strangers in the land of Egypt."[73]

Judging from the way conversion candidates are often treated in many Jewish communities, it seems that most interpret this mitzvah to apply only after the person has completed her conversion. However, from the moment Ruth had decided to convert, Scripture credited her with the same status as Naomi, as it states, "They both walked until they came to Bethlehem…"[74] Likewise, in the description of Avraham and Yitzchak; after Yitzchak had become aware that he was to be sacrificed, Scripture states, "They both walked together."[75] This is to teach us that Yitzchak's willingness to be sacrificed matched Avraham's willingness to sacrifice him, and they both walked together with an equal heart.[76] Similarly, the Midrash emphasizes the preciousness of the conversion candidate, since Ruth was compared to Naomi in righteousness, even before she could formalize her conversion in front of the rabbinical court.

---

[72] *Shemot* 23:9.
[73] *Devarim* 12:19.
[74] *Megillat Ruth* 1:19.
[75] *Bereishit,* 22:8.
[76] Rashi, ibid.

אמר ר' אבהו בוא וראה כמה חביבין גרים
לפני הקב"ה כיון שנתנה דעתה להתגייר השוה
הכתוב אותה לנעמי שנאמר ותלכנה שתיהן עד
בואנה בית לחם: (ילקוט שמעוני רות, א:תרא)

Rabbi Abahu said, Come and see how precious
proselytes are to the Holy One, blessed be He. Once
she [Ruth] had **set her heart on converting**, Scripture
placed her in the same rank as Naomi, as it is said,
"They both walked till they came to Bethlehem"
(*Yalkut Shimoni Ruth* 1:601).

Chapter Five

From Barley to
Wheat

משעורה לחיטה

At the Beginning of the Barley Harvest
בתחילת קציר השעורים

וַתָּשָׁב נָעֳמִי וְרוּת הַמּוֹאֲבִיָּה כַלָּתָהּ עִמָּהּ הַשָּׁבָה
מִשְּׂדֵי מוֹאָב וְהֵמָּה בָּאוּ בֵּית לֶחֶם בִּתְחִלַּת קְצִיר
שְׂעֹרִים: (רות א:כב)

"Naomi and Ruth the Moabitess, her daughter-in-
law, returned from the fields of Moav, and they came
to Bethlehem at the beginning of the barley harvest"
(*Megillat Ruth* 1:22).

Ruth arrived in Israel at the beginning of the barley harvest, in
order to compare her to the Jewish people, whose purification
process also began then. Both Ruth's and Israel's transformation
began during the time of the barley harvest, just prior to
Pesach. By converting at this time, Ruth became exactly like
Israel who were like converts at Sinai in the wake of the Exodus
from Egypt. G-d brought forth from Ruth the glory of the
Kingdom of Israel in a way that alluded to the Jewish people,
so that no-one should be astounded how something so sweet
came forth from Moav–a people so detrimentally opposed to
the values of Israel. וּמֵעַז יָצָא מָתוֹק–"Out of the strong came
forth sweetness."[73] The Kingdom of Israel did not derive from
a born daughter of Israel. Rather, Ruth, who came from the
impure people of Moav, personified the people of Israel, who

---

[73] *Shoftim* 14:14.

were also sunken in the impurity of the Egyptian idols prior to the Exodus. Just as Hashem purified the children of Israel from the impurity of Egypt, and converted them to become the Jewish people, so did He cleanse Ruth from the dross of Moav, in order to bring forth from her the root of David.[74]

Ruth's Refinement Process Reflected in Nature
הטבע משקפת את תהליך ההזדככות של רות

וַתִּדְבַּק בְּנַעֲרוֹת בֹּעַז לְלַקֵּט עַד כְּלוֹת קְצִיר
הַשְּׂעֹרִים וּקְצִיר הַחִטִּים וַתֵּשֶׁב אֶת חֲמוֹתָהּ:
(רות ב:כג)

"So she stayed close to the maidservants of Boaz and gleaned until the barley harvest and the wheat harvest were finished, then she returned to her mother-in-law" (*Megillat Ruth* 2:23).

The three-month period from the beginning of the barley harvest starting in Nissan (the month of Pesach), until the culmination of the wheat harvest at the end of Sivan (the month of Shavuot) reflects the purification process of the Jewish people, whom Hashem purified from the Egyptian idolatry. It takes three months to remove previous impure attachments and grow into a new person steeped in holiness. This parallels the three months period it takes for the features of a fetus to be fully formed.[75] Consequently, there exists a law that a convert needs to wait three months before getting married.[76]

---

[74] Rabbi Moshe Alshich, *Megillat Ruth* 1:22.
[75] *Babylonian Talmud, Berachot* 60a.
[76] The reason for this halacha is to verify that the child is conceived from Jewish parents. "A female convert, who were married before she converted needs to wait. We even separate a converted couple for ninety days in order to distinguish between seed that is sown in holiness from seed that is not sown in holiness" (*Shulchan Aruch, Eben Ha'ezer* 13:5). Today, when pregnancy tests can be verified, rabbis may permit converts to marry prior to three months after conversion (*Shut Achiezer* 4:48, *Shut Shevet HaLevi*, 8:8, 8:74).

Egypt is compared to a bleeding woman, who must count seven days before immersing in a mikvah to become ritually pure for her husband. Likewise, during the seven weeks between the Exodus from Egypt and receiving the Torah, we get purified while counting the Omer. The Omer is the measurement of barley, which was offered during this purification period. Since we were sunken into the forty-nine gates of impurity in Egypt,[77] our purification sacrifice was specifically barley, which is animal food as Rashi explains.

שעורים-ולא חטים (סוטה יב) היא עשתה מעשה
בהמה וקרבנה מאכל בהמה: (רש"י, במדבר ה:טו)

The offering of the *sotah*[78] is from barley and not wheat because she did an animalistic deed; therefore, her offering is from animal food (Rashi, *Bamidbar* 5:15).

We gradually refine ourselves during the Omer period until we reach ultimate purification and perfection on Shavuot when we offer two loaves of wheat bread, which represent refined human food.[79] The process of refinement of the Jewish people and of Ruth reflects the process of nature during the Omer period. There is a deep inherent connection between the ripening of our surrounding nature and our own inner spiritual and emotional growth. The barley harvest takes place during early spring when everything in nature begins to bloom. The counting of the Omer from Pesach to Shavuot, elevating and rectifying our character, is a ripening process that culminates on Shavuot, in our ability to receive the Torah and become complete. Between the barley and wheat harvest, most of the fruits in Israel are ripening on

---

[77] *Zohar Chadash, Parashat Yitro, Article Why the Exodus is Mentioned Fifty Times.*
[78] A married woman suspected of adultery. See *Bamidbar* 5:12-15.
[79] *Likutei Halachot, Hilchot Netilat Yadayim for the Meal,* halacha 6:34. *Likutei Halachot* written *by* Rabbi Nathan (1780-1844), the leading disciple of Rabbi Nachman of Breslau, explains the halachot of the *Shulchan Aruch* in the light of Rabbi Nachman's Chassidic insights. *Sefat Emet* for Shavuot 5637. Rabbi Yehuda Aryeh Leib Alter, (1847-1905), Gora Kalwaria (Ger), Poland, *Admor* of Gur. *Sefat Emet* on the Torah, distinguished by the profundity of their ideas and clarity of exposition, reflects the marked influence of the Maharal of Prague.

the tree, ready to be picked soon after the giving of the Torah. Likewise we, the fruits of Hashem's creation, go through a maturing process, becoming ready to be picked as Hashem's bride on Shavuot. While the apricots, peaches, plums, apples and grapes are budding, flowering and gradually ripening to become the perfect fruit, we likewise go through the process of perfecting the attributes of the Tree of Life. These characteristics include kindness, restraint, splendor, endurance and empathy.[80]

The Hebrew word for completion as in "...עַד כְּלוֹת קָצִיר"– "until the completion of the harvest,"[81] is related to the word כָּל which means all.[82] This word also means bride and hence daughter-in-law, as in, "...וְרוּת הַמוֹאֲבִיָּה כַלָּתָה"– "...Ruth the Moabitess, her daughter-in-law...."[83] A bride can be compared to a fully ripened fruit picked by her husband. She has completed herself to the extent that she is ready to enter a new stage in life as a married woman. Likewise, both the Jewish people and Ruth completed themselves to the extent that they were ready to be picked by Hashem and enter a new stage in life by receiving the Torah.

The Mitzvot of the Field   מצוות השדה

The kindness we exhibit toward the poor and weak is the major distinction between human beings and the animal kingdom, where 'survival of the fittest' is the rule. This is why the Torah juxtaposes counting the Omer (animal food), and offering the

---

[80] The seven weeks between Pesach and Shavuot, when we count the Omer, correspond to the seven lower *sefirot* – the emotional manifestations. They also represent aspects of the human personality. The first week during the holiday of Pesach corresponds to *chesed* – kindness, the second week to *gevurah* – restraint. These are followed by *tiferet* – splendor, *netzach* – endurance, *hod* – empathy, *yesod* – foundation, and culminate in *malchut* – royalty in conjunction with the holiday of Shavuot.
[81] *Megillat Ruth* 2:23.
[82] The root כל is mentioned 29 times in *Megillat Ruth*.
[83] *Megillat Ruth* 1:22.

two loaves of wheat bread on Shavuot (human food), with
the commandment for the landowner to provide for the poor
through three different mitzvot of the field.

עַד מִמָּחֳרַת הַשַּׁבָּת הַשְּׁבִיעִת תִּסְפְּרוּ חֲמִשִּׁים יוֹם
וְהִקְרַבְתֶּם מִנְחָה חֲדָשָׁה לַהֹ': מִמּוֹשְׁבֹתֵיכֶם
תָּבִיאוּ לֶחֶם תְּנוּפָה שְׁתַּיִם שְׁנֵי עֶשְׂרֹנִים
סֹלֶת תִּהְיֶינָה חָמֵץ תֵּאָפֶינָה בִּכּוּרִים לַהֹ':
וּבְקֻצְרְכֶם אֶת קְצִיר אַרְצְכֶם לֹא תְכַלֶּה
פְּאַת שָׂדְךָ בְּקֻצְרֶךָ וְלֶקֶט קְצִירְךָ לֹא תְלַקֵּט
לֶעָנִי וְלַגֵּר תַּעֲזֹב אֹתָם אֲנִי הֹ' אֱלֹהֵיכֶם:
(ויקרא כג:טז-כב)

"You must count fifty days until the day after the
seventh week, then you shall bring a new grain offering
to Hashem. You shall bring from your settlements two
loaves of bread as a wave offering; each shall be made
of two-tenths of a measure of fine flour; they shall be
baked leavened; they are the first fruits to Hashem…
and when you reap the harvest of your land, you shall
not reap all the way to remove the corner of the field,
or gather the gleaning of your harvest; you shall leave
them for the poor and for the stranger: I am Hashem
your G-d" (*Vayikra* 23:16-22).

The Three Mitzvot of the Field Mentioned in *Megillat Ruth*
שלושת מצוות השדה הנזכרות במגילת רות

פאה – *Peah:* **Corner** – As the farmer is harvesting his field, he
is commanded not to harvest the crops growing at the edge of
the field, so that the poor people can come and pick their share.[84]

---
[84] *Vayikra* 19:10.

לקט – *Leket*: **Leaving Fallen Stalks while Reaping** – As the produce is reaped, individual stalks often fall to the ground. The Torah commands us to leave them on the ground, so that the poor can walk behind the harvester and pick up the sheaves he drops.[85] *Leket* only applies when less than three sheaves fall together.[86]

שכחה – *Shichecha*: **Leaving the Forgotten Bundles** – When the produce has been piled in bundles, the farmer may not go back to collect a forgotten bundle. It must be left in the field for the needy.[87] Rashi explains that these Mitzvot of the Field are of such importance that they are mentioned both in *Vayikra* 19:9 and repeated in *Devarim* together with the list of holidays, in order to teach us that keeping them is compared to building the Temple and sacrificing on it.

...אמר רבי אבדימי ברבי יוסף מה ראה הכתוב ליתנם באמצע הרגלים פסח ועצרת מכאן וראש השנה ויום הכפורים וחג מכאן ללמדך שכל הנותן לקט שכחה ופאה לעני כראוי מעלין עליו כאילו בנה בית המקדש והקריב עליו קרבנותיו בתוכו: (רש"י, ויקרא כג:כב)

...Rabbi Abdima, the son of Rabbi Yosef said, What reason had Scripture to place it [the law concerning the corner of the field] amidst those regarding the festival sacrifices – those of Pesach and Shavuot on one side of it, and those of Rosh Hashana, Yom Kippur and Sukkoth following on its other side? To teach you that he who leaves the gleanings, the forgotten bundle, and the corner of the field to the poor as it ought to be, is regarded as though he had built the Temple and offered his sacrifices therein (Rashi, *Vayikra* 23:22).

---

[85] *Vayikra* 23:22.
[86] See Rashi, *Vayikra* 19:9.
[87] *Devarim* 24:19.

We can now understand why the Kingdom of Israel and the root of Mashiach, who will build the Temple, come about specifically through the Judean landowner Boaz offering the poor widow, Ruth, to glean in his field.

Gleaning – Raising up the Fallen Sparks
לקט – להעלות ניצוצות נפולים

וַתְּלַקֵּט בַּשָּׂדֶה עַד הָעֶרֶב... (רות ב:יז)

"She gleaned in the field until the evening…" (*Megillat Ruth* 2:17).

Ruth does not collect forgotten stacks of sheaves; neither does she harvest the corners of the field. From the three ways the Torah provides for the poor, Ruth chose exclusively to glean. Ruth was gleaning much more than the sheaves of barley and wheat. Ruth was picking up everything that everyone else had left behind and dropped. By returning to glean in the Land of Israel, Ruth was elevating not only the soul of her deceased husband, but also the souls of Elimelech's entire household who left the Holy Land during times of trouble. Moreover, through her acts of selfless *chesed*, Ruth was elevating the entire Jewish people to become worthy to merit her Messianic offspring.

Winnowing – Final Refinement   זריה – זיקוק סופי

וְעַתָּה הֲלֹא בֹעַז מֹדַעְתָּנוּ אֲשֶׁר הָיִית אֶת נַעֲרוֹתָיו
הִנֵּה הוּא זֹרֶה אֶת גֹּרֶן הַשְּׂעֹרִים הַלָּיְלָה: (רות ג:ב)

"Now there is Boaz our kinsman, with whose young women you were. Behold, he is winnowing barley tonight on the threshing floor" (*Megillat Ruth* 3:2).

Winnowing is the act of separating the chaff and other undesirable parts from the grain by means of a current of air. The process of winnowing uses the wind to blow the seeds from their husk. One method is to throw the plant upward to the wind so that the husks fall separately and the seeds can be gathered. Ruth and Boaz had to endure their optimal refinement process, much like that which is described above, in order to merit becoming the forbearers of the Mashiach. In addition to growing spiritually during the period of progressing from the barley to the wheat harvest, Boaz was also rising from harvesting to winnowing, which entails separating the chaff from the kernels. This is an act symbolizing his personal refinement, which made him suitable to perform the great rectification with Ruth.

Chapter Six

Wisdom and Modesty:
Perfection of Intellect and Character

חכמה וצניעות

*W*ise and Modest   חכמה וצנועה

The same day that Ruth was divinely guided to glean in the field of Boaz, divine supervision brought Boaz to visit his land, where he immediately noticed Ruth.

וַיֹּאמֶר בֹּעַז...לְמִי הַנַּעֲרָה הַזֹּאת? (רות ב:ה)

"Boaz asked... 'whose young woman is this?'" (*Megillat Ruth* 2:5).

We would never expect Boaz, a *talmid chacham* (Torah scholar), the head of the Sanhedrin, and a man of extraordinary religious piety, to pay attention to a woman. Rashi intuited the peculiarity of Boaz's inquiry and implied that Boaz's question was prompted by Ruth's extraordinary acts of righteousness, which were too apparent to go unnoticed.

למי הנערה הזאת-וכי דרכו של בועז לשאול
בנשים אלא דברי צניעות וחכמה ראה בה
שתי שבלים לקטה שלשה אינה לקטה והיתה
מלקטת עומדות מעומד ושוכבות מיושב כדי
שלא תשחה: (רש"י, רות ב:ה)

"TO WHOM IS THIS YOUNG WOMAN?" – Is it the way of Boaz to inquire about women? Behold, he noticed matters of modesty and wisdom in her. She would glean two sheaves but not three. She would glean those standing upright in an upright position, and those lying in a sitting position, in order that she would not have to bend (Rashi, *Megillat Ruth* 2:5).

Malbim notes that Boaz didn't ask, "Who is this young woman?" but rather "to whom…" implying, "Who is worthy to marry this outstanding young woman?" Since she is so special in her modesty, I am inquiring about her. The Midrash highlights even more the details of Ruth's acts of modesty.

למי הנערה הזאת ולא הוה חכים לה אלא
כיון שראה אותה נעימה ומעשיה נאים התחיל
שואל עליה כל הנשים שוחחות ומלקטות וזו
יושבת ומלקטת כל הנשים מסלקות כליהם
וזו משלשלת כליה כל הנשים משחקות עם
הקוצרים וזו מצנעת עצמה כל הנשים מלקטות
בין העמרים וזו מלקטת מן ההפקר... (מדרש
רבה רות, ד:ו)

"Whose young woman is this?" Did he not recognize her? When he saw, however, that she was pleasing, and her conduct was pleasing he began to inquire about her. All the other women tucked up their clothes; she let hers hang down. All the other women flirted with the reapers; she acted modestly. All the other women gathered between the sheaves; but she only gathered from the discarded grain… (*Midrash Ruth Rabah* 2:6).

Boaz noticed that Ruth personified a perfect balance of intellectual and moral perfection. Most of the gleaners were not well-versed in the halacha that permits the poor to glean only one or two fallen sheaves that fall together. Even those who knew this halacha, did not find it important enough to exert themselves in order to keep the letter of the law. Ruth was the only gleaner who not only knew the halacha, but moreover, had the moral impetus to apply it meticulously. In addition, she behaved with the utmost modesty and care to avoid inadvertently being seen in an inappropriate pose during the strenuous process of gleaning.

Boaz noticed that Ruth's mind and heart were connected. She put her Torah learning into practice in acts of righteousness, and she mastered the highest level of body awareness, having conscious control over even her smallest physical movement. Perhaps the reason why Rashi mentions modesty before wisdom, and then proceeds to describe her acts of wisdom first, is to teach us that modesty (moral perfection) and wisdom are intertwined, as it is written, "An unlearned person cannot be pious."[85] Indeed, Ruth's wisdom was integrated with her modesty. She did not try to grab more than her share but was content with the modest allotment for the gleaners. Yet, it is impossible to act modestly without having wisdom such as foresight and the higher consciousness of mind/body awareness. Similarly, it is impossible to be wise without having the moral perfection to desire the way of truth, even when that knowledge is opposed to one's personal interest.

Modesty requires Foresight
צניעות דורשת ראיית הנולד

וַתֵּלֶךְ וַתָּבוֹא וַתְּלַקֵּט בַּשָּׂדֶה... (רות ב:ג).

"She went, and she came and gleaned in the field…" (*Megillat Ruth* 2:3).

Why is it necessary to write both "She went, and she came"? How would it be possible to come without first going? According to Rashi, based on the Midrash, Ruth actually went back and forth from her place to the field twice, in order to ensure that she would be able to find her way back in the dark.

---

85 *Pirkei Avot* 2:5.

ותבא ותלקט בשדה-מצינו במדרש רות עד לא
אזלת אתת שהוא אומר ותבא ואחר ותלקט
אלא שהיתה מסמנת הדרכים קודם שנכנסה
לשדה והלכה ובאה וחזרה לעיר כדי לעשות
סימנים וציונים שלא תטעה בשבילין ותדע
לשוב. (רש"י, רות ב:ג)

...She would mark the ways before she entered
the field, and she would go and return to the city,
in order to make signs, so she wouldn't get lost on
the way, and she would know how to return...
(Rashi, *Megillat Ruth* 2:3).

Ruth's "marking her ways" is another example of how Ruth's
wisdom and foresight merged with the morality of her
modesty. Ruth was concerned to avoid any situation that may
be conducive to improper male/female interaction. It was clear
to her that a woman alone and lost in the dark can easily be
taken advantage of by corrupt and immoral men. Therefore,
she took preemptive measures to ensure that she would be
able to find her way back even at night. This is why she went
and came again the same way several times to mark the path,
in order that she would not get lost in the dark.

Kindness and Faith   חסד ואמונה

When Boaz offered his protection to Ruth as a gleaner, he
explained that he had already been told about her greatness.

וַיַּעַן בֹּעַז וַיֹּאמֶר לָהּ הֻגֵּד הֻגַּד לִי כֹּל אֲשֶׁר
עָשִׂית אֶת חֲמוֹתֵךְ אַחֲרֵי מוֹת אִישֵׁךְ וַתַּעַזְבִי
אָבִיךְ וְאִמֵּךְ וְאֶרֶץ מוֹלַדְתֵּךְ וַתֵּלְכִי אֶל עַם אֲשֶׁר
לֹא יָדַעַתְּ תְּמוֹל שִׁלְשׁוֹם: (רות ב:יא)

"For I have surely been told about everything you
have done for your mother-in-law after the death of
your husband, how you left your father, and mother
and the land of your birth, and came to a people you
have not known before" (*Megillat Ruth* 2:11).

The word הֻגַּד–"it has been told" is repeated to indicate that
Boaz had been made aware of Ruth's two different kinds of
outstanding deeds: one of moral action, and the other of
spiritual perception.

The first deed was Ruth's exceptional kindness to her mother-
in-law, clearly not for the sake of pleasing her husband,
since he was no longer alive, but because of her quality of
selflessness. This indicates that Ruth's good-heartedness rose
beyond nature, since there is naturally tension between a
daughter-in-law and her mother-in-law. Ruth's extraordinary
kindness made her worthy to be a true daughter of Israel, as
kindness is one of the three main characteristics of a Jew.[86]

The second deed was how Ruth left her biological parents and
her familiar surroundings, in order to take refuge under the
wings of the *Shechinah* (Divine Feminine Indwelling Presence).
Alshich notes that in the order of the verse, it mentions that
Ruth left her parents prior to leaving her birthplace. She had
already left her parents spiritually by deciding to become
Jewish, before she actually departed from them physically.
Boaz recognized that Ruth's following Naomi to the Land of
Israel, and hence her conversion, was for the sake of Heaven,
being that this is where G-d's wings shelter more than in all
other countries ruled by the ministering angels.[87]

---

[86] *Babylonian Talmud, Yevamot* 49a.
[87] Ramban, Rabbi Moshe ben Nachman – Nachmanides, (1194-1270),
Catalonia, Spain. His Torah commentary was first to incorporate teachings of
Kabbalah, *Vayikra* 18:25.

Physical and Spiritual Perfection

שלמות גשמית ורוחנית

יְשַׁלֵּם הָשֵׁם פָּעֳלֵךְ וּתְהִי מַשְׂכֻּרְתֵּךְ שְׁלֵמָה מֵעִם
הָשֵׁם אֱלֹהֵי יִשְׂרָאֵל אֲשֶׁר בָּאת לַחֲסוֹת תַּחַת
כְּנָפָיו: (רות ב:יב)

"May Hashem repay your deed and may your reward
be complete from Hashem the G-d of Israel under
Whose wings you have come to seek refuge"
(*Megillat Ruth* 2:12).

Boaz's blessings to Ruth correspond to the two kinds of perfection
he recognized in her: physical and spiritual. Corresponding to
her kindness toward her mother-in-law, he said, "May Hashem
repay your deed," wishing for her a physical reward for her
tangible actions. Corresponding to her conversion, he said,
"May your reward be complete from Hashem the G-d of Israel
that you have come to seek refuge under His wing." Meaning
that she should receive a spiritual reward to parallel her spiritual
act of conversion, as this is the most complete reward.[88] These
words of Boaz teach us that there is no greater reward than being
in the dynamic process of continually seeking out Hashem.

Since the accomplishments of mitzvot are beyond what can be
encapsulated into any tangible reward, our Sages teach us that
"there is no reward for a mitzvah in this world,"[89] and "the reward
of a mitzvah is another mitzvah."[90] Ruth's powerful desire to cleave
to Hashem was her greatest reward. Ruth found favor in Boaz's
eyes both because of her spiritual perception and steadfast belief
in cleaving to the G-d of Israel, and because of her altruistic acts
of kindness, showing that her spiritual perception was anchored
in physical action, as the highest manifestation of spirituality is
to extend oneself for the sake of someone else's physical needs.

---

[88] Malbim, *Megillat Ruth* 2:12.
[89] See *Babylonian Talmud, Kidushin* 39b and *Chulin* 142a.
[90] See *Tana d'Bei Eliyahu Rabah* 15, *Pirkei Avot* 4:2.

Chapter Seven

Megillat Ruth and the Holiday of Shavuot

מגילת רות והג השבועות

We were all Converts   כולנו היינו גרים

Every Shavuot we read the Scroll of Ruth to remind ourselves
that we, too, were converts when we received the Torah at
Mount Sinai. The Talmud teaches us that the souls of the future
righteous converts were actually there, with us at Mount Sinai,
and received the Torah together with us.[91] Therefore, we must be
careful not to discriminate against righteous converts. Although
Hashem chose the Jewish people and gave us the Torah, we
are still required to be ready to embrace the righteous converts
who cleave to us, as the Torah commands, "You must love the
stranger, for you were strangers in Egypt."[92] Reading about Ruth
on Shavuot reminds us that we are surely not superior to Ruth
who elevated herself from the society most opposed to the Torah
way, to become a righteous convert cleaving to the Torah of Israel.

Rabbi Nathan of Breslau explains that we read *Megillat Ruth*
on Shavuot, because the time of the giving of the Torah is most
appropriate for converts and *Ba'alei Teshuva*.[93] After having
left the impurity of Egypt for the holiness of Israel, all of the
Jewish people were like converts, beginning to come close to

---

[91] "But not with you alone…" (*Devarim* 29:13). "…but with those who are
here" (Ibid. 14). I have only those who were currently standing on Mount
Sinai. From where do we learn about the future generations and the converts
that would convert in the future? Scripture teaches us, "And those who are not
here with us today" (Ibid.). (*Babylonian Talmud, Shavuot* 39a).

[92] *Devarim* 10:19.

[93] Rabbi Nathan, *Likutei Halachot, Laws of Converts*, 3.

their Father in Heaven. For this reason the revelation at Sinai included the sound of the Shofar, fire and torches, which comprise the aspect of judgment, in order to burn the negative energy that was attached to the Jewish people from the impurity of Egypt. It is interesting to note that the sound of the shofar is often associated with ingathering converts and those dispersed in exile. For this reason, prior to blowing the shofar on Rosh Hashana, we recite *Tehillim* 47, which mentions converts.[94]

Sefat Emet explains that the Jewish people were created in order to extract holy sparks from the entire world through the merit of learning Torah.[95] If we are worthy, we will attract converts by means of the strength of our Torah learning alone. If we are unworthy, we will have to be dispersed in exile in order to gather converts.[96] This is alluded to in the words of the prophet, "O Hashem, my strength, and my stronghold, and my refuge in the day of affliction, nations shall come to you from the end of the earth..."[97] The words for strength and stronghold derive from the Hebrew word עֹז/*oz* referring to the strength of Torah. Elimelech, who was not worthy, had to leave the Land of Israel in order to bring forth the soul of King David and Mashiach through Ruth. However, the holy soul embodied by Ruth, the righteous convert, came on her own to Boaz, through the power of his Torah learning, as his name testifies. Boaz (בֹּעַז –in him is strength)–the strength of the Torah. This concept is alluded to in the language, אֲשֶׁר בָּאת – "that you have come,"[98] with which Boaz praised Ruth for coming on her own to the Land of Israel, to seek refuge under the wings of G-d.[99]

---

[94] "The nobles of the peoples are gathered together, the people of the G-d of Avraham" (*Tehillim* 47:10).
[95] *Sefat Emet on the Torah, Parashat Yitro,* 5638.
[96] Rabbi Elazar said, The Holy One did not exile Israel among the nations except in order to add converts, as it states, "I will sow her to me in the earth" (*Hoshea* 2:25). A person only sows a *se'ah* in order to produce several *kor*... (*Babylonian Talmud, Pesachim* 87b). A *kor* is equal to 30 *se'ah*; a *se'ah* equals approximately 8.3 liters (8.8 quarts).
[97] *Yirmeyahu* 16:19.
[98] *Megillat Ruth* 2:12.
[99] See *Midrash Ruth Rabbah* 5:4 quoted in chapter 4. **Ruth and Yitro.**

When the holy sparks come on their own without being extricated, they can achieve an even greater ascent. The elevation that can be accomplished by the power of the Torah gives us a clue to why we sacrifice two loaves of *chametz* (leavened) bread on Shavuot. Throughout the year, all other meal offerings are made from *matzah*, since *chametz* symbolizes the *yetzer hara* (evil inclination).[100] It is only on Shavuot, at the time of the giving of the Torah, that we sacrifice *chametz* bread, in order to hint to the fact that the power of the Torah gives us the ability to raise up the entire creation.[101]

Connecting the Written with the Oral Torah
חבור תורה שבכתב עם תורה שבעל פה

We read the scroll of Ruth on Shavuot to establish the fact that Hashem gave Moshe both the Written and the Oral Torah on the sixth day of the Hebrew month, Sivan. The Torah teaches us that Moshe stayed on Mount Sinai for forty days and forty nights before descending with the two tablets of the Ten Commandments.[102] How could it be necessary to spend forty days just to receive the two Tablets with the Ten Commandments? It makes sense that during those forty days on the mountain, Hashem taught Moshe the entire Written and Oral Torah.[103]

The story of Ruth is read at the time of the giving of the Torah so that we might know that the Written and the Oral

---

[100] *Ba'al Haturim,* Rabbi Ya'acov ben Asher, (1269-1343), Cologne, Germany, the author of *Arba'ah Turim,* commentary on the Torah, based on *gematria* and scriptural word patterns, *Vayikra* 2:11.

[101] *Sefat Emet, Bamidbar,* for Shavuot year 5659.

[102] *Shemot* 24:18, 34:28.

[103] Rashi *Vayikra* 25:1,*Vayikra* 26:46; *Gur Aryeh* (Maharal), Rabbi Yehuda Loew ben Betzalel, (1520-1609), Prague, Talmudic scholar, Jewish mystic and philosopher, served as the Chief Rabbi of Prague, best known for his super-commentary, the *Gur Aryeh,* on Rashi's Torah commentary, *Vayikra* 25:1.

Torah, are interdependent, and it is impossible to understand one without the other. Indeed David, the anointed of G-d unto all generations, was descended from a Moabite woman, whose Jewish legitimacy depends on the Oral Torah.[104] The entire people of Israel is supported on the foundations of the House of David, yet without the Oral Torah, King David and Mashiach would not even be Jewish, since their ancestor Ruth, the Moabitess, would never have been able to convert.[105] It is only through the Oral Torah that it becomes clear that a Moabite woman is permitted to convert, because women are not expected to go out into the field and approach strangers with bread and water.[106] Likewise, the Torah teaches that Sarah was modest inside of her tent.[107] Still, David's Jewishness was indeed questioned until the Oral interpretation of the Torah, "Moabite but not Moabitess," finally became completely ascertained and accepted by all.[108]

---

[104] Rabbi Eliyahu Kitov, (1912-1976), Warsaw, Poland – Israel, *The book of the Heritage*, Shavuot, page 105.

[105] See *Devarim* 23:4-5 which states that Moabites are not allowed to convert because they did not bring the Jewish people bread and water, when they were traveling through their land in the desert.

[106] "All the honor of the king's daughter is within" (*Tehillim* 45:14)... It is written "an Ammonite" but not an Ammonitess, "a Moabite" but not a Moabitess (*Devarim* 23:4)...Rabbi Shimon says, "Because they did not approach you with bread and water," (Ibid. 5) – It is the way of a man to approach, but it is not the way of a woman to approach... (*Babylonian Talmud Yevamot* 77a).

[107] *Bereishit* 18:9.

[108] During David's time, Doeg the Edomite said, "Before asking whether he is worthy for kingdom, we should ask whether he is worthy to enter the Jewish congregation." "Why would he not be worthy?" "Because he comes from Ruth the Moabitess." Avner said to him, "They have taught in the Mishna, 'An Ammonite, but not an Ammonitess, a Moabite but not a Moabitess.'" Doeg retorted, "From now on you will say, 'Mamzer but not Mamzeress?'" Avner answered, "Mamzer is not a noun, but a descriptive clause meaning, 'there is a strange blemish,' this applies equally to men and women." Doeg asked, "Perhaps you will say 'An Egyptian but not an Egyptianess?'" Avner answered, "Here it is different since Scripture gives an explicit reason, 'because they did not approach you with bread and with water' (*Devarim* 23:5). It is the way for a man to approach but not the way for a woman." Doeg answered, "The men should approach the men, and the women the women." Avner was silenced... "Go ask in the Beit Midrash." He asked and they told him, "An Ammonite but not an Ammonitess, a Moabite but not a Moabitess" (*Babylonian Talmud, Yevamot* 76b).

The Hardships of Torah   יסורים למען התורה

Everything worthwhile is acquired through effort and difficulty. We all know the expression, 'Easy Come Easy Go.' In order to achieve anything important in life, we need to first prove our worthiness. Since there is nothing more valuable than the Torah, in order to deserve it, we may be tested with difficulties and hardships.

> ומה ענין רות אצל עצרת שנקראת בעצרת בזמן
> מתן תורה, ללמדך שלא נתנה תורה אלא על
> ידי יסורין ועוני וכה"א חיתך ישבו בה תכין
> בטובתך לעני אלה על ידי יסורין ועוני וכה"א
> חיתך ישבו בה תכין בטובתך לעני אלהים:
> (ילקוט שמעוני רות, א:תקצו)

> Why do we read the Scroll of Ruth during Shavuot at the time of the giving of the Torah? It is to teach us that the Torah was only given by means of suffering and poverty as it states, "Your flock found a dwelling in it: You, O G-d prepare of your goodness for the poor"[109] (*Yalkut Shimoni Ruth* 1:596).

Just as Ruth, a princess from birth, became a pauper gleaning in the fields for the sake of cleaving to the Torah, so must we show willingness to go through thick and thin for the sake of the Torah. The pleasure we receive through drinking from the wellsprings of Torah, and from living a pure spiritual life, greatly outweigh the material sacrifices. As King David exclaimed, "Your Torah is better for me than a thousand gold and silver pieces."[110] Poverty and hardships lead to humility, a prerequisite for receiving the Torah. As the Midrash states, "If those involved in Torah learning are wealthy, they may become haughty, but if they are aware of their hunger they

---

[109] *Tehillim* 68:11.
[110] *Tehillim* 119:72.

will remain humble."[111] Haughtiness does not leave a space for the Torah to penetrate, as the haughty person is full of himself. On the other hand, through humility, we may open ourselves to encompass Torah. Therefore, Moshe, the receiver of Torah, was known to be the most humble of all men.[112] Likewise, Ruth, the mother of Mashiach, who will anchor the Torah in the hearts of the world, showed ultimate humility and self-sacrifice. Once she had proven herself worthy of the Torah, she became elevated from gleaning in the fields, to become the mistress of the land, as the wife of Boaz, the wealthy land owner and Torah scholar. He himself had endured the poverty of famine without deserting his people. When Hashem sees that we are willing to go through hardship for the sake of His Torah, poverty has then served its purpose, and is no longer necessary for our spiritual purification. This explains why Rabbi Yochanan says, "Whoever learns Torah through poverty will eventually learn it through wealth."[113]

The Torah of Mashiach   תורת המשיח

Another connection between *Megillat Ruth* and Shavuot is that King David, Ruth's great grandson, who integrated Torah to the very essence of his being, was born and passed away on Shavuot. There are three crowns in the world: The crown of *Kehuna* (Priesthood), the crown of Kingship and the crown of Torah.[114] King David only received the crown of Kingship for the sake of his Torah, since the Jewish kingdom must be based on the Torah to the highest degree. Therefore, we read the Scroll of Ruth, which culminates in David's genealogy, on Shavuot at the time of the giving of the Torah. This in order

[111] *Midrash Ruth Zutra,* parasha 1.
[112] *Bamidbar* 12:3.
[113] *Pirkei Avot* 4: 9.
[114] Based on *Babylonian Talmud, Yoma* 72b.

to elucidate that the reason David merited Kingship was only by means of the crown of his Torah.[115] Likewise, Mashiach, a direct descendant of King David, will reflect the Kingdom of Hashem on earth through his deepest integration of the Torah within our physical world. We are supposed to look forward to the Messianic era[116] and the elevated consciousness it will bring when "the land will be full of the knowledge of G-d."[117] However, it is hard for us to imagine what this G-d consciousness entails. How can we look forward to something without knowing what exactly it entails? Therefore, we read *Megillat Ruth* about the birth of King David, the sprout of Mashiach, to help us to connect the spiritual experience of the Torah Revelation with the future elevated G-d consciousness, which we will soon experience at the advent of King Mashiach. By means of our collective memory of the spiritual pleasure that we experienced at Mount Sinai, we have a model for what we are looking forward to with the arrival of the Mashiach.[118]

Connecting Torah with *Tefilah* (Prayer)
לחבר בין תורה לתפילה

Receiving the Torah is linked to prayer, as the purpose of prayer is to become a vessel to receive divine influence. Therefore on Shavuot, we sacrifice two loaves of bread corresponding to Torah and *tefilah*. *Sefat Emet* explains[119] that we read *Megillat Ruth* on Shavuot in order to connect Torah with *tefilah,* which together constitute the complete reception of the Torah, נַעֲשֶׂה וְנִשְׁמָע– "We will do and we will hear."[120] Torah, which we receive from

---

[115] *Kedushat Halevi, Drush for Shavuot.*

[116] Rambam, Rabbi Moshe ben Maimon – Maimonides, (1135-1204), Egypt, the most influential Jewish thinker of the Middle Ages, author of the first systematic code of Halacha, the *Mishneh Torah, Laws of Kings*, chapter 11:1.

[117] *Yesha'yahu* 11:9.

[118] *Kedushat Halevi, drush* for Shavuot.

[119] *Sefat Emet on the Torah*, for Shavuot 7643.

[120] *Shemot* 24:7.

above, corresponds to נִשְׁמָע–hearing. Whereas prayer initiated by us, corresponds to נַעֲשֶׂה–doing. Prayer is also the aspect of deed, because the action of donning *tzitzit*, *tefillin* and giving *tzedaka* (charity) precedes it.

Because we blemished נַעֲשֶׂה – deed, on the sixth of Sivan,[121] which corresponds to וְנִשְׁמָע–hearing,[122] we need to repent by means of prayer during Shavuot. Therefore, it is customary to recite the entire prayerful book of *Tehillim* on Shavuot. The connection between Torah and *tefilah* is also highlighted in the Scroll of Ruth, where the deeds of Ruth and Boaz were the preparation for Oved, their son, whose name means "to worship or pray." Their deeds are compared to the *tzedakka* and *tzitzit* preceding prayer.

The Power of Prayer   כח התפילה

עַל עַ"ז שְׁתֵּי נָשִׁים מָסְרוּ עַצְמָן עַל שֵׁבֶט יְהוּדָה
תָּמָר וְרוּת תָּמָר הָיְתָה צוֹעֶקֶת אַל אֵצֵא רֵיקָנִית
מִן הַבַּיִת וְרוּת כָּל שָׁעָה שֶׁחֲמוֹתָהּ אוֹמֶרֶת לָהּ לְכִי
בִּתִּי הָיְתָה בּוֹכָה שֶׁנֶּאֱמַר וַתִּשֶּׂנָה קוֹלָן וַתִּבְכֶּינָה
עוֹד: (רות א:י"ד); (מדרש זוטא רות, פרשה א)

Two women gave over their soul for the sake of the tribe of Yehuda, Tamar and Ruth. Tamar would cry out, "Let me not go out empty-handed from this house." Ruth, whenever her mother-in-law told her, "Go, my daughter" she would cry. As it states, "They lifted their voices and they cried more" (*Megillat Ruth* 1:14; *Midrash Zuta Ruth*, parasha 1).[123]

---

[121] When we made the golden calf immediately following the revelation at Sinai on the sixth of Sivan.

[122] Shavuot is the aspect of נִשְׁמָע – hearing, because on that day we heard, received and accepted the Ten Commandments.

[123] See also *Yalkut Shimoni Ruth* 1:601, quoting *Megillat Ruth* 1:9.

Why, according to the Midrash does "They lifted their voice and cried" refer to Ruth alone? Didn't both Ruth and Orpah cry? A close reading of the text reveals that although tears streaked both of the sisters' faces, actually only one of them cried from her heart, while the other dropped crocodile tears. Alshich notices that the Hebrew word "וַתִּשֶּׂנָה" – "lifting their voice in crying" is missing the *alef*.[124] This alludes to the fact that one of them did not truly lift her voice in prayerful crying. Orpah's crying was very short-lived and only lasted two seconds until she kissed her mother-in-law goodbye, as written in the continuation of the verse. Yet, Ruth's cry from the depths of her being, reverberating in the heart of "the sweet singer of Israel," David. He beseeched Hashem through his *Tehillim*, when he cried out, "מִמַּעֲמַקִּים קְרָאתִיךָ הֵשֵׁם" – "From the depths I called out to you Hashem."[125] As a result of Ruth's heartfelt crying, David was able to testify about himself "וַאֲנִי תְפִלָּה" – "I am prayer."[126]

The entire tribe of Yehuda, to which David belonged, is known for the power of their prayer, as it states, "This is the blessing of Yehuda, and he said, 'Hear, Hashem, the voice of Yehuda…'"[127] The name Yehuda itself means "to praise," which is the peak of prayer. We can understand why Elimelech (from the tribe of Yehuda) was punished so severely for deserting his people during the time of famine, as the role of the tribe of Yehuda is to precede their prayer for Israel with acts of kindness and *tzedaka*. Moreover, Elimelech corresponds to the letter *yud* in Hashem's name,[128] which also alludes to the hand that gives.[129] Finally, the quintessence of Kingdom is to be a channel for

---

[124] See Alshich, *Megillat Ruth* 1:14. Compare also with *Megillat Ruth* 1:9 וַתִּשֶּׂאנָה קוֹלָן וַתִּבְכֶּינָה.

[125] *Tehillim* 130:1.

[126] *Tehillim* 109:4. See also this book, chapter 1. *From Ruth to David*, p. 18.

[127] *Devarim* 33:7.

[128] See this book, chapter 4. **Righteous Convert**, *The meaning of the name Ruth*, p. 39.

[129] The word *yud* has the same letters as the word *yad* which means hand. In addition, the shape of the letter resembles an outstretched hand.

divine influence in the world, as Kingdom has nothing on its own.[130] Through deeds of *tzedaka* and kindness to Ruth, Boaz (also from the tribe of Yehuda) merited to rectify Elimelech and build the kingdom in Israel.

Torah of Kindness   תורת חסד

דרש ר' שמלאי תורה תחלתה גמילות
חסדים וסופה גמילות חסדים תחילתה
גמילות חסדים דכתיב ויעש השם אלהים.
לאדם ולאשתו כתנות עור וילבישם וסופה
גמילות חסדים דכתיב ויקבר אותו...
(תלמוד בבלי מסכת סוטה דף יד/א)

Rabbi Zimlai expounded, "The Torah begins and ends with bestowing kindness. Its beginning is the bestowal of kindness as it states, 'Hashem, G-d made for man and his wife coats of skin and clothed them.'[131] Its end is bestowal of kindness as it states, 'He buried him…'" [Moshe][132] (*Babylonian Talmud, Sotah* 14a).

G-d's purpose in creation was to bestow of His goodness to another.[133] The Torah, which is the blueprint of creation,[134] therefore reflects *chesed*; its highest purpose. The Scroll of Ruth, likewise, centers around *chesed* which is mentioned three times in connection with Hashem's blessing.[135]

---

[130] לית לה מגרמה כלום Arizal, *Sefer Halikutim, Parashat Teruma*, chapter 26.
[131] *Bereishit* 3:21.
[132] *Devarim* 34:6.
[133] Rabbi Moshe Chaim Luzzatto, Ramchal, Padua, Italy, (1707-1746), prominent Kabbalist and philosopher, *Derech Hashem*, chapter 2:1.
[134] See *Midrash Bereishit Rabbah* 1:1, *Zohar* 1:24b, BEREISHIT – "With *reishit*, [meaning Torah] Hashem created the Heavens and Earth;" and "Hashem looked into the Torah and created the world" (*Zohar, Teruma* 161b).
[135] *Megillat Ruth* 1:8, 2:20, 3:10.

...יעשה השם עמכם חסד... א"ר זעירא מגלה
זו אין בה לא טומאה ולא טהרה ולא איסור
ולא היתר ולמה נכתבה ללמדך כמה שכר
טוב לגומלי חסדים: (מדרש רבה רות, ב:יד)

"May G-d do kindness to you..."[136] Rabbi Seira said, "This Scroll does neither contain [laws of] impurity nor laws of purity, neither prohibitions nor permissions. Why was it written? To teach how great is the reward for those who bestow kindness" (*Midrash Ruth Rabbah* 2:14).

In the beginning of the *Megillah* we are introduced to Elimelech and his family, who left the Land of Israel during the famine, without sharing their wealth and bestowing kindness upon their fellow Jews. They deserted Israel to the Land of Moav, which was known for its lack of kindness. It was there that Elimelech and his sons eventually met their death. Ruth, Machlon's widow, rectified Elimelech's family's lack of *chesed*. Although she descended from the Moabite people, who were the antithesis to Israel in their lack of *chesed*, Ruth was the precious hidden pearl redeemed from the refuse of Sodom. All her deeds were beyond the letter of the law.[137] In her self-effacing kindness to sustain her mother-in-law both physically and spiritually (by restoring the soul of her lost son) she embodied Hashem's ultimate *chesed* manifested in the Torah. We, therefore, read *Megillat Ruth* on Shavuot to remind us of the central role of *chesed* within the Torah, which is also called the Torah of Kindness.[138]

---

[136] Ibid. 1:8.
[137] *Midrash Ruth Rabbah* 7:6.
[138] *Mishlei* 31:26.

Chapter Eight

The Mitzvah of Levirate Marriage (Yibum)

מצוות יבּוּם –
חסד של אמת

*T*he Mitzvah from the Torah

מצות יבום מהתורה

The highest kindness a person can perform according to the Torah is kindness to the dead,[139] as one can expect nothing in return for this kind of benevolence. The Torah teaches us that if one of two brothers dies childless, the mitzvah of *yibum* (levirate marriage) requires the widow and the surviving brother to marry each other. This mitzvah entails the greatest kindness to the deceased brother, as the first child born from this union will be called in his name.

כִּי יֵשְׁבוּ אַחִים יַחְדָּו וּמֵת אַחַד מֵהֶם וּבֵן אֵין
לוֹ לֹא תִהְיֶה אֵשֶׁת הַמֵּת הַחוּצָה לְאִישׁ זָר יְבָמָהּ
יָבֹא עָלֶיהָ וּלְקָחָהּ לוֹ לְאִשָּׁה וְיִבְּמָהּ: וְהָיָה הַבְּכוֹר
אֲשֶׁר תֵּלֵד יָקוּם עַל שֵׁם אָחִיו הַמֵּת וְלֹא יִמָּחֶה
שְׁמוֹ מִיִּשְׂרָאֵל: (דברים כה:ה-ו)

"When brothers live together, and one of them dies without a son, the wife of the deceased shall not be married to a strange man. Her husband's brother shall unite with her, and take her as his wife and perform the duty of a husband's brother to her (*yibum*). It shall be that the firstborn son that she bears shall establish the name of his deceased brother, and his name shall not be erased from Israel" (*Devarim* 25:5-6).

---

[139] See Rashi on *Bereishit* 47:29.

84

The first time the mitzvah of *yibum* is mentioned in the Torah is when Yehuda tells his second son Onan to marry Tamar, the wife of his deceased brother Er, in order to establish seed for him.

וַיֹּאמֶר יְהוּדָה לְאוֹנָן בֹּא אֶל אֵשֶׁת אָחִיךָ וְיַבֵּם
אֹתָהּ וְהָקֵם זֶרַע לְאָחִיךָ: (בראשית לח:ח)

"Then Yehuda said to Onan, 'Go unto your brother's wife, and perform the duty of *yibum* with her, and raise up seed to your brother'" (*Bereishit* 38:8).

Yibum is not mentioned directly in *Megillat Ruth*, but is alluded to in several places through the language of redemption.[140] Redemption is indeed the underlying theme of the book of Ruth, both on the individual level through the mitzvah of *yibum,* and on a cosmic level, leading to the birth of David, the foundation for the ultimate redemption. The beginning of chapter two in *Megillat Ruth* sets the stage for the mitzvah of *yibum*, by introducing Boaz as a relative to Naomi and Elimelech. This is confirmed by Naomi's exclamation of joy when she finds out that the field in which Ruth has been gleaning belongs to none other than Boaz.

וַתֹּאמֶר נָעֳמִי לְכַלָּתָהּ בָּרוּךְ הוּא לַהֲשֵׁם אֲשֶׁר לֹא
עָזַב חַסְדּוֹ אֶת הַחַיִּים וְאֶת הַמֵּתִים וַתֹּאמֶר לָהּ
נָעֳמִי קָרוֹב לָנוּ הָאִישׁ מִגֹּאֲלֵנוּ הוּא: (רות ב:כ)

"Naomi said to her daughter-in-law, 'Blessed be he of Hashem, who did not abandon His kindness to the living or to the dead.' For Naomi explained to her, 'The man is related to us; he is one of our redeeming relatives'" (*Megillat Ruth* 2:20).

When Naomi discerned Hashem's supervision leading Ruth to the field of her close relative, Boaz, she is jubilant with renewed hope, as he has the ability to restore and raise up the name of her deceased son.

---

[140] *Megillat Ruth* 2:1, 2:20, 3:2, 3:9, 3:12, 4:1-10, 4:14.

The Redemption of *Yibum*   גאולת היבום

The mitzvah of *yibum* is shrouded in mystery. How exactly does a person "raise up seed" for his deceased brother? Why is it specifically the fulfillment of this mitzvah by Tamar and Yehuda, together with Ruth and Boaz, that gives birth to the redeemer of Israel? Ramban explains that *yibum* is one of the great hidden secrets which the ancient Sages knew even before the revelation of the Torah. According to the Midrash,[141] Yehuda was the first to begin the mitzvah of *yibum*. He received its secret from his father.

...יש תועלת גדולה ביבום האח, והוא הראוי להיות קודם בו ואחריו הקרוב במשפחה, כי כל שארו הקרוב אליו ממשפחתו אשר הוא יורש נחלה יגיע ממנו תועלת... הנהיגו לפנים בישראל לעשות המעשה הזה בכל יורשי הנחלה, באותם שלא יהיה בהם איסור השאר, וקראו אותו גאולה, וזהו ענין בועז וטעם נעמי והשכנות והמשכיל יבין: (רמב"ן, בראשית לח:ח)

...Considerable benefit accrues through the brother who performs the levirate duty, and he, therefore, takes precedence over all the others. After him comes the closest of kin [to do *yibum*], for there derives an advantage from any close kin of the family of the deceased, who is in line to inherit his property.... The Sages made it customary in Israel that any close kin who inherits the property should do this deed, if they are not prohibited by any of the incestuous prohibitions [of the Torah]. They called it 'redemption,' and this is the story of Boaz and the reason that the neighbors of Naomi [said, "A child is born to Naomi"] (Ramban, *Bereishit* 38:8).

---

[141] *Bereishit Rabbah* 85:5.

The great benefit of the mitzvah of *yibum* entails that the closest relative has the ability to bestow his deceased brother with spiritual offspring through levirate marriage. The first child from this union belongs spiritually to the person for whom *yibum* was performed. This is why Onan, in his selfishness, refused to impregnate Tamar, as he realized that the child would not be his in the spiritual sense.

וַיֵּדַע אוֹנָן כִּי לֹא לוֹ יִהְיֶה הַזָּרַע וְהָיָה אִם בָּא
אֶל אֵשֶׁת אָחִיו וְשָׁחֵת אַרְצָה לְבִלְתִּי נְתָן זֶרַע
לְאָחִיו: (בראשית לח: ט)

"Onan knew that **the seed would not be his:** and it came to pass, when he joined with his brother's wife, that he spilled it on the ground, **without giving seed** to his brother" (*Bereishit* 38:9).

The importance of spiritual eternity used to be much more clearly ingrained in our awareness. Today, it is hard for us to connect to the mitzvah of marrying for the sake of bestowing eternal life to the closest relative, through the spiritual child born in his name. However, in reality, to be willing to marry for the sake of helping someone else is one of the greatest possible kindnesses. We do have the capacity to learn to love for the sake of a mitzvah.[142] The widow has the ability to procure a child for her late husband through the closest relative, because she became "one flesh" with her husband. Even after his demise, she still has part of his soul within her. Moreover, the soul of her late husband derives from the same root as his closest relative. When these two join together with pure intention to bestow eternal life to the deceased, they conceive a child who will continue in the place of his father, as *Sefer Hachinuch* explains.[143]

---

[142] I believe this is the main message of the 2012 Israeli drama film *Fill the Void* written and directed by Rama Burshtein.

[143] *The Book of Education*, thirteenth century, Spain, is a popular medieval work that systematically enumerates the six hundred and thirteen mitzvot (based upon Maimonides' system of counting) and explains them from both a legal and moral perspective.

...מִשָּׁרְשֵׁי הַמִּצְוָה, לְפִי שֶׁהָאִשָּׁה אַחַר שֶׁנִּשֵּׂאת
לְאִישׁ הֲרֵי הִיא כְּאֶחָד מֵאֵבָרָיו, שֶׁכֵּן יְחַיֵּב
הַטֶּבַע מִפְּנֵי מַעֲשֵׂה הָאָב הָרִאשׁוֹן שֶׁלּוּקְחָה אַחַת
מִצַּלְעוֹתָיו וּמִמֶּנָּה כּוֹנְנָה לוֹ הָאֵל אִשָּׁה, וְהָאִישׁ
הַזֶּה שֶׁמֵּת בְּלֹא בָנִים שֶׁיִּהְיוּ חֵלֶק מִמֶּנּוּ לְזִכָּרוֹן
לוֹ וְלִמְלֹאות מְקוֹמוֹ בָּעוֹלָם לַעֲבוֹדַת בּוֹרְאוֹ, וְעוֹד
אֵין זֵכֶר לוֹ בָּעוֹלָם הַגּוּפָנִי זוּלָתִי זֹאת הָאִשָּׁה
שֶׁהִיא עֶצֶם מֵעֲצָמָיו וּבָשָׂר מִבְּשָׂרוֹ, הָיָה מֵחַסְדֵּי
הָאֵל עָלָיו לְהָקִים לוֹ זֶרַע מִמֶּנָּה עַל יְדֵי אָחִיו
שֶׁהוּא גַם כֵּן כַּחֲצִי בְּשָׂרוֹ, כְּדֵי שֶׁיִּהְיֶה אוֹתוֹ
הַזֶּרַע מְמַלֵּא מְקוֹמוֹ וְעוֹבֵד בּוֹרְאוֹ תַּחְתָּיו וְיִזְכֶּה
עַל יָדוֹ בָּעוֹלָם הַנְּשָׁמוֹת אֲשֶׁר הוּא שָׁם, כְּמוֹ
שֶׁיָּדוּעַ דְּבָרָא מְזַכֶּה אַבָּא שֶׁכֵּן אָמְרוּ זִכְרוֹנָם
לִבְרָכָה [סַנְהֶדְרִין קי"ד ע"א] בְּרָא מְזַכֶּה אַבָּא:
(סֵפֶר הַחִנּוּךְ, מִצְוָה תקצ"ח)

"...After a woman is married to a man, she becomes as one of his limbs, for so nature has ordained through the experience of the first father, [Adam] one of whose ribs was taken by G-d, and fashioned into a woman. This is also in order to allow part of the man who dies childless to survive as his memorial and take his place in serving his Creator. He has no other memorial in this physical world except for this woman, who is bone of his bone and flesh of his flesh. It is a divine act of kindness to allow him to reproduce children through his brother, who is also like part of himself. In this way, the child will take his place and serve his Creator in his stead. He will, therefore, derive merit in the World of Souls, where he remains. As they said, "A son requires merit for his father"[144] (*Sefer Hachinuch,* Mitzvah 598).

[144] *Babylonian Talmud, Sanhedrin* 104a.

"Your Brother's Wife"   "אשת אחיך"

The mitzvah of *yibum* seems to contradict the Torah prohibition against having relations with the brother's wife. How can the Torah command the husband's brother to marry his widow when the Torah reading for Yom Kippur clearly forbids a person from having relations with his brother's wife?

עֶרְוַת אֵשֶׁת אָחִיךָ לֹא תְגַלֵּה עֶרְוַת אָחִיךָ הִוא:
(ויקרא יח:טז)

"You shall not uncover the nakedness of your brother's wife; it is the nakedness of your brother" (*Vayikra* 18:16).

The Talmud teaches us a great principle about Torah law: For every Torah prohibition, there is always a one-time dispensation. This helps us overcome the human inclination that desires to disobey the mitzvot. The awareness that there is a possible way out makes it psychologically easier to stay within the boundaries. For example, if a person has a craving to eat milk and meat together, he may then eat a cow's udder, which is kosher. Similarly, desiring someone else's wife is prohibited, but a man can marry a woman who was previously married. In the same manner, there is an exception from the prohibition of not marrying the brother's wife, in the situation when levirate marriage applies.[145] Not only does *yibum* override the prohibition against joining with his brother's wife; it even becomes a mitzvah when performed correctly with proper intention. Should a man die childless, the Torah puts aside the prohibition of marrying the brother's wife, for the sake of performing the mitzvah of *yibum*, by marrying his brother's widow. However, the mitzvah of *yibum* is very intricate and thus the entire tractate *Yevamot* in the Talmud is devoted to discussing its many details.[146] Furthermore, the obligation

---

[145] *Babylonian Talmud, Chulin* 109b.
[146] *Yevamot* is the plural form of the word *yibum*.

must be fulfilled with the proper intention. If a man marries
the wife of his deceased brother for her beauty or with any
motive other than in order to establish seed for his brother,
then he not only fails to fulfill his obligation, but according
to the Sage Abba Shaul he is even bordering on an actual
violation of the prohibition of marrying a brother's wife.

דתניא אבא שאול אומר הכונס את יבמתו
לשם נוי ולשום אישות ולשום דבר אחר כאילו
פוגע בערוה וקרוב אני בעיני להיות הולד ממזר:
(תלמוד בבלי מסכת יבמות דף לט/ב)

Abba Shaul says, someone who marries his sister-in-
law for her beauty, to have a wife, or for any other
purpose, is as if he has committed an immoral
relationship, and I am close to saying that the child
will be a *mamzer*[147] (*Babylonian Talmud, Yevamot* 39b).

Already during Talmudic times, it was no longer possible to
perform the mitzvah of *yibum* with the correct intention.
Therefore, in order to avoid any possibility of violating the
prohibition of marrying the brother's wife, it was preferred
to perform *chalitza*, (the loosening of the shoe ritual) also
described in *Devarim*, chapter 25, instead of *yibum*.[148]

מצות היבום קודמת למצות חליצה בראשונה
שהיו מתכוונין לשם מצוה ועכשיו שאין מתכוונין
לשם מצוה אמרו מצות חליצה קודמת למצות
יבום... (תלמוד בבלי מסכת בכורות דף יג/א)

The mitzvah of *yibum* was originally preferred over
the mitzvah of *chalitza* when they were able to have
intention for the sake of the mitzvah, but now when
we do not intend for the sake of the mitzvah, they
said the mitzvah of *chalitza* is preferred over the
mitzvah of *yibum* (*Babylonian Talmud, Bechorot* 13a).

---

[147] An illegitimate child conceived through one of the forbidden relationships.
[148] For further explanation see *Chalitza – Loosening the Shoe* on pp. 95-97.

The intention needed to perform the mitzvah of *yibum* is, according to the *Zohar*,[149] encoded within the words of the mitzvah itself, "The name of the deceased shall not be erased from Israel."[150] The word "name" does not refer to a formal, technical and legalistic process, but rather, it is a description of the *kavanah* (mental intention) and inner, spiritual meaning of the mitzvah. The intention of the man who marries his deceased brother's wife must be that "the name of the deceased shall not be erased from the world." Therefore, the mitzvah of *yibum* is the expression of the ultimate spiritual refinement; distinguishing between two identical external actions only through the internal intention.[151]

Selflessness to the Highest Degree
מסירת נפש בדרגה העילאית

In our generation, it is almost impossible to relate to the mitzvah of *yibum*. In the modern world, people marry for 'love,' which usually is expressed first through infatuation and attraction, followed by spiritual compatibility only as an afterthought. In the Torah, the order is reversed. Only after our Patriarch Yitzchak marries Rivkah does he begin to love her.[152] This teaches us that we *do* have the ability to make ourselves feel attraction and love for the person we have decided to marry for spiritual reasons. This kind of rational love engenders lasting relationships, unlike those who fall in and out of love. Nevertheless, it was established by the Sages since Talmudic times that today we are not on the level to perform the mitzvah of *yibum*, since we are unable to reach the level of selflessness necessary for having the proper intention required to fulfill this mitzvah.

---

[149] *Zohar* 1:155b.
[150] *Devarim* 25:6.
[151] See Rabbi Shabtai Teicher, *The Old Man and the Sea*.
[152] *Bereishit* 24:67.

Likewise, the anonymous 'redeemer' in the Scroll of Ruth, who was a closer relative than Boaz, was unable to reach this level of selflessness. Therefore, he refused to marry Ruth. A close look at the text describing his refusal, reveals that his concern was similar to Onan's (that the child would not be his). There is an emphasis on the words pertaining to the self.

וַיֹּאמֶר הַגֹּאֵל לֹא אוּכַל לִגְאָול **לִי** פֶּן אַשְׁחִית אֶת
נַחֲלָ**תִי** גְּאַל לְךָ אַתָּה אֶת גְּאֻלָּ**תִי** כִּי לֹא אוּכַל
לִגְאֹל: (רות ד:ו)

"The redeemer said, 'I cannot redeem it **for myself**, lest I destroy **my own** inheritance; you take over the right of **my** redemption; for **I** cannot redeem it'" (*Megillat Ruth* 4:6).

The 'redeemer' is considered selfish in his refusal to marry Ruth because he was concerned about tainting his lineage (*yichus*) and good family name by marrying a 'questionable' convert.[153] Ironically, it is exactly because he was concerned about his own name that he remains nameless throughout the *Megillah*. This teaches us a powerful message: one should not be overly concerned with lineage when choosing a marriage partner. Marrying a convert without *yichus* procured the royal name of David,[154] while the name of the man who refused to marry a convert is left out and entirely forgotten. His nickname, "Ploni Almoni," means 'covered and concealed.'

Rashi explains that Almoni means 'unknown' (without name) because he was silent to the words of Torah. He should have accepted the ruling, "A Moabite but not a Moabitess."[155] But he said, "Lest I destroy my inheritance."[156]

---

[153] *Megillat Ruth* 4:6.
[154] See *Megillat Ruth* 4:18-22 where Ruth's prestigious lineage is traced all the way to the birth of King David.
[155] See also this book, chapter 1. **From Ruth to David**, Blemished Lineage?
[156] *Megillat Ruth* 4:6, see also Rashi, *Megillat Ruth* 4:1.

Perhaps it's possible to compare Ploni Almoni's reluctance to
marry Ruth, with the many Jews today who avoid marrying
righteous converts. Like Ploni Almoni, they are concerned
about *yichus* still needing to integrate the lessons of *Megillat
Ruth* into their lives.

The *Megillah* continues with a peculiar statement describing
the customary practice of transactions in Israel in former days.

וְזֹאת לְפָנִים בְּיִשְׂרָאֵל עַל הַגְּאוּלָה וְעַל הַתְּמוּרָה
לְקַיֵּם כָּל דָּבָר שָׁלַף אִישׁ נַעֲלוֹ וְנָתַן לְרֵעֵהוּ וְזֹאת
הַתְּעוּדָה בְּיִשְׂרָאֵל: וַיֹּאמֶר הַגֹּאֵל לְבֹעַז קְנֵה לָךְ
וַיִּשְׁלֹף נַעֲלוֹ: (רות ד:ז-ח)

"Now this was the custom in former times (*lefanim*) in
Israel, in cases of redemption or exchange: to validate
any transaction, one would take off his shoe and give
it to the other. Such was the practice in Israel. So when
the redeemer said to Boaz, 'Acquire it for yourself,' he
removed his shoe" (*Megillat Ruth* 4:7-8).

Ploni Almoni's inability to achieve the purity of intention
required to fulfill the mitzvah of *yibum* is evident from the
above quote from *Megillat Ruth*,[157] which conveys his refusal
to marry Ruth. With the words, "I cannot redeem for myself,
lest I destroy my own inheritance." Ploni Almoni explained
that he was unable to attain the intention required to fulfill
the mitzvah of *yibum*. Therefore, marrying Ruth would be
considered as if he uncovered the nakedness of his brother's
wife. The redeemer then turned to Boaz and said, "Redeem for
you my redemption," for he knew that only Boaz the *tzaddik*
would be able to perform the redemption properly. This
statement is juxtaposed to the verse " ...THIS WAS לְפָנִים/

[157] The *Maor VaShemesh*, Rabbi Kalonymus Kalman HaLevi Epstein, (1753-
1823), Krakow, *Allusions of Ruth*. Rabbi Epstein was a child prodigy and a
great and G-dly Kabbalist. His commentary on the Torah and the five *Megillot*
is one of the fundamental works of Chassidism.

LEFANIM IN ISRAEL—because the word *lefanim* can refer
to the inner meaning[158] IN CASES OF REDEMPTION
of *yibum*, which redeems the soul of the dead so it can rest.
OR EXCHANGE—in order that the soul will be established
and have rest, it needs to be redeemed from the world of
exchange[159] and brought into this world. "TO VALIDATE
ANY TRANSACTION A PERSON WOULD TAKE OFF
HIS SHOE—Taking off one's shoe alludes to removing one's
physical being, as when Moshe Rabbeinu was told at the
burning bush, "Take your shoe off your foot."[160] He would
remove his physical being AND GIVE IT TO HIS FRIEND
—to become completely self-sacrificing (*mesirut nefesh*) to
Hashem who is called "his friend." As it states, "Your friend
and your father's friend," etc.[161]

THE REDEEMER SAID TO BOAZ, ACQUIRE IT FOR
YOURSELF, AND HE TOOK OFF HIS SHOE—It is not
clear who took off whose shoe. There are those who say that
Boaz gave his shoe to Ploni Almoni, and there are those who
say that Ploni Almoni gave his shoe to Boaz, as it states in the
Talmud.[162] It is possible to explain that it refers to both. It can
refer to Ploni Almoni when he separated himself temporarily
from his physical being with the help of Boaz, who brought
him to this holy level momentarily, in order to teach him the
intention required in this mitzvah. It can also refer to Boaz
the *tzaddik*, who surely separated himself completely from his
physical being, in order to draw down a soul for the child
conceived through this holy *yibum*.

The Maor VaShemesh gives us a glimpse of Boaz's holy
intention. This ability to operate completely for the sake of

---

[158] From the root פ-נ-מ – as in the word פנימיות – the inner meaning.
[159] The world where the souls exist prior to reincarnation is referred to as 'exchange.'
[160] *Shemot* 3:5. For more details regarding this concept, see this chapter, The Shoe of the Soul.
[161] *Mishlei* 27:1.
[162] *Babylonian Talmud, Baba Metzia* 47a.

Hashem without any hint of personal desire is reflected no less in his holy soul-mate, Ruth, who offered herself to Boaz, completely and totally *l'shem shamayim* (for the sake of heaven). This is why Boaz praised Ruth and called her willingness to perform *yibum* with him an even greater *chesed* than all of her collected self-sacrifice supporting her mother-in-law.[163]

We can now attempt to understand why it is particularly the mitzvah of *yibum* that conceives the redeemer of Israel. Hashem created the world for the sake of *chesed*[164] and requires us to emulate His ways.[165] It makes sense therefore that the Mashiach, the human being who is the most perfected actualized image of G-d, will be conceived through the mitzvah which requires and expresses the highest *chesed* possible, to the extent of transcending one's physical being. Performing *yibum*, the ultimate kindness of truth, was called 'redemption,' since it redeemed the deceased from spiritual death. Therefore, King David, the redeemer of Israel, descends from the union of *yibum* that Boaz performed with Ruth through the highest most altruistic and spiritual intention.

Chalitza–Loosening the Shoe

חליצה–חילוץ הנעל

The Torah provides an alternative for the person who was unable or unwilling to marry his brother's widow. Even during biblical times, not everyone was on the level to perform the mitzvah of *yibum*. Today, we are even further from being able to attain the proper intention to marry solely for the sake of bestowing kindness toward another. Therefore, in our time,

---

[163] *Megillat Ruth* 3:10.
[164] "For I have said, 'The world is built through *chesed*...'" (*Tehillim* 89:3). See also Ramchal, *Derech Hashem* chapter 2, *Sefer Hayashar*, gate 1, *Torat Moshe* on *Bereishit* 14:19-12, *Akeidat Yitzchak* 12:3.
[165] *Shemot* 15:2, *Devarim* 28:9, Babylonian Talmud, *Shabbat* 133b.

yibum is prohibited and the standard practice is to perform a ritual in which the man's shoe is removed in a ceremony called *chalitza* (loosening of the shoe).

וְאִם לֹא יַחְפֹּץ הָאִישׁ לָקַחַת אֶת יְבִמְתּוֹ וְעָלְתָה יְבִמְתּוֹ הַשַּׁעְרָה אֶל הַזְּקֵנִים וְאָמְרָה מֵאֵן יְבָמִי לְהָקִים לְאָחִיו שֵׁם בְּיִשְׂרָאֵל לֹא אָבָה יַבְּמִי: וְקָרְאוּ לוֹ זִקְנֵי עִירוֹ וְדִבְּרוּ אֵלָיו וְעָמַד וְאָמַר לֹא חָפַצְתִּי לְקַחְתָּהּ: וְנִגְּשָׁה יְבִמְתּוֹ אֵלָיו לְעֵינֵי הַזְּקֵנִים וְחָלְצָה נַעֲלוֹ מֵעַל רַגְלוֹ וְיָרְקָה בְּפָנָיו וְעָנְתָה וְאָמְרָה כָּכָה יֵעָשֶׂה לָאִישׁ אֲשֶׁר לֹא יִבְנֶה אֶת בֵּית אָחִיו: וְנִקְרָא שְׁמוֹ בְּיִשְׂרָאֵל בֵּית חֲלוּץ הַנָּעַל: (דברים כה:ז-י)

"But if the man does not want to marry his brother's widow, then his brother's widow shall go up to the gate to the elders and declare, 'My husband's brother refuses to establish a name in Israel for his brother; he will not perform the levirate duty with me.' Then the elders in the city shall summon him and speak to him. If he insists saying, 'I do not want to marry her,' then his brother's widow shall approach him in the presence of the elders, and loosen his shoe from off his foot. And she shall spit in his presence and declare, 'So shall be done to the man who will not build up his brother's house.' And his name shall be called in Israel, 'The house of him that had his shoe loosened'"(*Devarim* 25:7-10).

According to Arizal the reason why the Torah requires the widow to spit in the presence of the person who refuses to perform *yibum* with her, is in order to release the part of her husband's spirit which undulates within her, so she can become free to marry any man.

והענין הוא כי כשאדם נושא אשה נותן בה חלק ממנו ממש וזה טעם וירקה בפניו וכשאדם רוקק

בהכרח משליך עם אותו רוק קצת רוח חיוני
ממנו. וזהו ענין וירקה בפניו שאותו רוח של
בעלה שהי' בה פורש ממנה ע"י אותו החליצה
ורקקיקה: (ספר טעמי המצוות, פרשת כי תצא)

...The matter is that when a person marries, he places
within her a real part of himself and when the person
spits, she emits with the spit part of the vital spirit
from him. This is the matter of "she shall spit in his
presence" the spirit of her husband within her separates
from her by means of this *chalitza* and spitting
(Arizal, *Ta'amei HaMitzvot, Parashat Ki Tetze*).

The Shoe of the Soul　　　　　　　　　נעל הנשמה

Malbim explains that the shoe symbolizes the physical body.
Just as the shoe encases the lowest part of the body and allows
it to ambulate in the world, so too does the body encase the
lowest level of the soul and allows it to manifest within the
physical world. Therefore, whenever G-d wants a person
to relate on a totally spiritual level, ignoring the body, He
commands him to remove his shoes. This applies to every Jew
on Yom Kippur. We ignore the physical for one day a year,
and to symbolize this, we remove our leather shoes. (Leather
specifically, because it comes from a living creature and hence
symbolizes the body in a much more graphic way than other
materials).[166] For this reason, G-d told Moshe to remove his
shoes at the burning bush,[167] and Yehoshua in Yericho, when
he first arrived in the Holy Land.[168] The Kohanim, likewise,
performed the holy service at the Temple in Jerusalem barefoot.

---

[166] Email article by Yosef Ben Shlomo Hakohen z"l.
[167] *Shemot* 3:5.
[168] *Yehoshua* 5:15.

In the case when *yibum* is not performed, the soul of the deceased is unable to stand a second time in the physical world, as if he remains without a 'shoe.' This is hinted by the widow removing the shoe of the person who did not perform *yibum* and calling his name "the house of releasing the shoe." This ritual signifies that he does not deserve physical comfort, or even a body, for that matter, since he refused to give a 'shoe,' i.e. physical form, to his deceased brother's soul that as a result lacks a physical body. Ruth hinted these concepts to Boaz by lying down on the threshing floor and uncovering his feet.[169] Her body language told him, "Since you are the redeemer to do *yibum*, therefore either reveal your feet to be without a shoe and be called 'the house of him that had his shoe released,' or allow me to lay besides you, to establish a name in Israel for my departed husband."[170]

Soul Elevation through the Mitzvah of *Yibum*
עלית הנשמה דרך מצות יבום

וְהָיָה הַבְּכוֹר אֲשֶׁר תֵּלֵד יָקוּם עַל שֵׁם אָחִיו הַמֵּת
וְלֹא יִמָּחֶה שְׁמוֹ מִיִּשְׂרָאֵל: (דברים כה:ו)

"It shall be that the firstborn son that she bears shall **establish the name** of his deceased brother and **his name shall not be erased** from Israel" (*Devarim* 25:6).

The mitzvah of *yibum* is the gateway into the awesome subject of *gilgulim* (reincarnations). It is known that the name of a thing is a description of its essence. Therefore, the Hebrew term for 'noun' is *shem-etzem*— 'the name of the essence.' Naming a child is an act of *ruach hakodesh* (divine inspiration). Every name is an accurate description of the soul mission and a sketch of the characteristics available to that person to help or hinder fulfillment of his mission.[171]

---

169 *Megillat Ruth* 3:14.
170 Malbim, *Megillat Ruth* 3:4.
171 Based on *Kol Hator*, chapter 3, as taught by Rabbi Shabtai Teicher z"l.

Since a name refers to one's essence, and a person's essence is his soul, the mitzvah of *yibum* accomplishes that **his soul** shall not be erased from Israel. The soul of his brother was on the verge of extinction, by not having succeeded in performing the mitzvah of begetting children. Hence, the act of *yibum* allowed that soul to get a second chance within this world. The child born from the union of *yibum* is actually the soul reincarnation of the person for whom *yibum* was performed.[172]

In the normal process of soul reincarnation, the three parts of the soul (*nefesh, ruach,* and *neshama*), must reincarnate separately in three different reincarnations. An even greater elevation of soul can be achieved through *yibum.* If a person is reborn in the secret of *yibum,* his previous body is considered as if it had never existed at all. For this reason, the entire *nefesh* returns as a new creation. It is possible, therefore, that the *ruach* and *neshama* can reincarnate together with the *nefesh* in the same lifetime, though not all at one time. At the time when he merits and performs mitzvot fitting for the *ruach,* then it will enter him, and it is the same with respect to the *neshama.*[173]

עוד יש חלוק אחר בבחי' הגלגול בעצמה אם
בענין המתגלגל בבחי' גלגול בכל גוף שיזדמן,
או במתגלגל ע"י אחיו, אשר זה נקרא סוד
היבום, והוא, כי כשבא בבחי' גלגול לכך,
הנה אינם מתגלים ביחד שלשתם הנר"ן, ולא
שניהם יחד, אלא הנפש לבדה עד שתתקן,
ואח"כ בגלגול אחר, הנפש והרוח לבדם, עד
יתוקן הרוח. ואח"כ בגלגול אחר, הנר"ן, עד
שתתקן הנשמה, ואז נשלמו גלגוליו כנז"ל. או
לפעמים כל אחד משלשתם יתגלגל לבדו בפני
עצמו כנז"ל. אבל כשמתגלגל ע"י אחיו, ובא
בסוד יבום, יכולים להתגלגל שם יחד שלשתם
הנר"ן: (שער הגלגולים, הקדמה ב)

---

[172] Arizal, *Etz Chayim* 11:6.
[173] Arizal, *Gate of Reincarnation* 3:7.

There is another difference between general reincarnation and reincarnation by means of his brother,
which is called "the secret of *yibum*." By general
reincarnation the three parts of a person's soul are not
reincarnated together; only the *nefesh* alone until it is
rectified. Afterwards, in a different reincarnation, the
nefesh with the *ruach* until the *ruach* is rectified, and
afterwards in another reincarnation all three, until the
neshama will become rectified, then his reincarnations
are completed However, when one is reincarnated
through his brother and comes in the secret of *yibum*,
the three parts of his soul can be reincarnated together
(Arizal, *The Gate of Reincarnations*, Introduction 2).

Malbim explains that the soul of the person who has passed
away without children has no rest and is still undulating
within his wife, waiting to bear fruit.[174] When his brother
performs *yibum* with her, the soul of the deceased returns a
second time to the world. Their child is indeed the departed
brother himself, who will be called in his name and take over
his inheritance of land. Therefore it states, "A son is born to
Naomi."[175] For Oved, the son of Boaz, was actually Machlon,
Naomi's son, reborn. The *Meshech Chachma*, quoting the
Zohar, makes an interesting observation regarding *yibum*.[176]
Since the child born from *yibum* is, in fact, the reincarnation
of the deceased, then the brother becomes his father, and the
wife his mother.

...אבל לענין הכוונה האלוקית כפי מה שביארו
בזוהר הקדוש (פ' וישב דף קפו), ורמב"ן
(בראשית לח, ח) שהוא סוד נשגב במחצב
הנפשות, וזה רמוז בפסוק (שם פסוק ט) וידע

---

[174] Malbim, *Megillat Ruth* 3:4, based on the *Zohar* 2:102a.
[175] *Megillat Ruth* 4:1.
[176] Rabbi Meir Simcha of Dvinsk, (The Ohr Sameach) (1843-1926),
Butrimonys, Lithuania, Rabbi of the *mitnagdim* (non-chassidic Jews) in the
Latvian town of Dvinsk.

אונן כי לא לו יהיה הזרע, ובמאמר השכנות
(סוף רות) יולד בן לנעמי, בזה אין המקרא יוצא
מידי פשוטו, דאינתתיה אימיה ואחוה אבוה:
(משך חכמה, דברים כה:ו)

However, the divine intention of the verse is according
to what is explained in the *Zohar*, (*Parashat Vayeshev*,
186) and Ramban (*Bereishit* 38:8). It is an awesome
secret concerning souls. This is indicated by the
verses, "Onan knew that the seed would not be his,"[177]
and "A child is born to Naomi."[178] In this respect,
the verse does not uproot the simple meaning. His
wife is his mother, and his brother is his father
(*Meshech Chochmah, Devarim* 25:6).

Yibum, Redemption and the Rise of the Feminine
מצות יבום, גאולה ועליית הנוקבא

What is the spiritual significance of the wife rising to become
her husband's mother through the process of *yibum*? As
explained, *yibum* brings about a twofold redemption, both to
the individual soul that receives a second chance in life, and to
our ultimate redeemer, the Mashiach, whose birth is a result
of this mitzvah. The concept of redemption is intrinsically
related to women. It is known that redemption takes place
in the merit of the righteous women,[179] rising from the small
point of the lowest *sefirah–malchut*, to a full stature with all ten
sefirot, as Arizal explains in his article about the diminishment

---

[177] *Bereishit* 38:9.
[178] *Megillat Ruth* 4:17.
[179] In the merit of the righteous women in that generation, Israel was
redeemed from Egypt (*Babylonian Talmud, Sotah* 11b), and in their merit
we will merit the future redemption (*Kav Hayashar*, chapter 82). The Arizal,
(*Sha'ar HaGilgulim, Hakdamah* 20) teaches that the future redemption will
follow the pattern of the Exodus. Thus we may assume that it will also come
as a result of the merit of righteous women.

of the moon.[180] We remain in exile as long as the light of the feminine is not completely evolved and revealed in the world.[181] Therefore, as the 'sun/son' of redemption rises, the archetype of the feminine grows from 'daughter' to 'mother.'

According to the Arizal, there are three different archetypes describing the evolvement of the feminine: 'daughter,' 'sister' and 'mother.' Through the mitzvah of *yibum,* the woman rises to her utmost elevation as the 'mother,' who is the nurturer of all life. Not only is she no longer dependent on man for her spiritual light as his 'mother,' she nurses and bestows light upon him as well. This reveals the secret of, "The woman of virtue is the crown of her husband."[182] In other words, her light shines above him and encompasses him.

ובזה תבין סוד מאמר ז"ל מאי בעטרה שעטרה
לו אמו, לא זז מחבבה עד שקראה אחותי, לא
זז מחבבה עד שקראה אשתי וכו'. כי בהיותה
אצלו שוה לו, אז היא אחותו, וכשהיא מזדווגת
עמו, נקראת אשתו. וכשהיא עולה במקום נה"י
דאמא... נקראת אמו, וזהו עטרת בעלה כנ"ל...
(פרי עץ חיים, שער מקרא קודש, פרק ב)

This is the secret of the saying of the Sages,[183] "He didn't stop loving her until he called her his sister..." For when she was equal to him then she is called his sister and when she rises to become mother, [then she becomes] "the crown of her husband" (*P'ri Etz Chayim, sha'ar mikra kodesh* 2).

---

[180] *Etz Chayim* 36:1.

[181] Rabbi Shlomo Elyashev (the *Leshem*) on the diminished moon. (See Sarah Yehudit Schneider, *Kabbalistic Writings on the Nature of Masculine and Feminine*).

[182] *Mishlei* 12:4.

[183] מהו בעטרה שעטרה לו אמו א"ל הן למלך שהיתה לו בת יחידה והיה אוהבה יותר מדאי לא זז מחבבה
עד שקרא אותה אחותו לא זז מחבבה עד שקרא אותה אמו כך היה הקב"ה מחבב את ישראל קראן
(שיר ה) אחותי רעיתי יונתי תמתי לא זז מחבבן עד שקראן אמו... (מדרש רבה במדבר יב:ח)
What is the meaning of "Upon the crown wherewith his mother has crowned him?" (*Shir Hashirim* 3:11). This is like a king who had an only daughter whom he loved too much. He didn't stop loving her until he called her his sister. He didn't stop loving her until he called her his mother... (*Midrash Bamidbar Rabbah* 12:8).

The womb of the mother in Hebrew, רֶחֶם/*rechem* also means mercy. Through the mitzvah of *yibum*, rather than judging the deceased husband for his past unfulfilled life, he receives mercy from the womb that provides him with a new opportunity for the future. In this way, *yibum* reflects the process of our future redemption in which G-d, in His great mercy, will redeem us from our current long-winded exile. No matter how unfruitful we have been in our lives, or how low we may have fallen, eventually Hashem will redeem us and extend us new life in the face of our past failures.

Chapter Nine

Soul-Reincarnations in the Book of Ruth

גלגולי נשמות
במגילת רות

$\mathcal{H}$idden Spark from Moav

ניצוץ צפון ממואב

וַתָּשָׁב נָעֳמִי וְרוּת הַמּוֹאֲבִיָּה כַלָּתָהּ עִמָּהּ הַשָּׁבָה
מִשְּׂדֵי מוֹאָב... (רות א:כב)

"Thus Naomi returned, and Ruth the Moabitess, her daughter-in-law, with her, returned from the fields of Moav…" (*Megillat Ruth* 1:22).

Ruth's entrance into the Land of Israel for the first time is described as returning. Since a person only returns to a place where he has previously been, we must ask, when did Ruth set her feet on the Holy Land of Israel prior to her "return" with Naomi? The answer is that Ruth was the reaper of the teachings of *chesed* that Avraham had implanted within Lot, his nephew. Several generations after Lot had separated from Avraham and from the Holy Land to settle in Moav, Ruth, a direct descendant of Lot, became a magnet for holiness. She cleaved to Avraham's spark of *chesed*, eventually returning it to its proper place in the Land of Israel. This is despite the fact that she was raised with the anti-*chesed* values and ingratitude that the people of Moav exemplified.[184] In the fields of Moav, there was no piety or *chesed*, except for one hidden gem, lost from its original owner, Avraham. Ruth embodied that gem

---

[184] When they did not offer bread and water to the descendants of Avraham to whom they owed their existence (*Devarim* 23:4-5). Ruth also rectified this ingratitude when she gleaned grains of sustenance for Naomi to whom she owed her spiritual existence.

of *chesed*, carrying on Lot's legacy from Avraham's home and preserving it through the refuse of Sodom and Moav. When Ruth converted to Judaism, her *chesed* had returned to its original source, as she "returned" in a spiritual sense to the place from where Lot deviated; into the fold of Avraham. Therefore, it states, "Her daughter-in-law, with her, who returned from the fields of Moav." In her sincere devotion to attach herself to Naomi, Ruth rectified Lot's separation from Avraham and eventually also Elimelech and his sons' lack of *chesed*. In Lot's greed for greener pastures and material goods, he was compelled to separate (הִפָּרֶד) from Avraham. The parallel language יַפְרִיד describing Lot's descendant, Ruth, in her cleaving to the people of Avraham, alludes to her rectification of Lot's separation.[185]

Lot's Daughter Encore   שיבת בת לוט

Every good deed, even thought and intention, is recorded above in order to eventually reap its reward. A good intention, without a proper deed accompanying it, must reincarnate into a body, which will complete the lofty intention with elevated deeds, according to Hashem's mitzvot. When Lot's daughter decided to conceive a child through her father, she had the purest of intentions. She thought that her father and sister were the only survivors in the world. So she acted out of selfless devotion for the sake of populating the earth. The purity of her intention is highlighted through the realization that most people's actions, even their righteous acts, are motivated by self-interest often masquerading as altruism. Yet, good intentions must be actualized by good deeds. Lot's daughter's good intention was by no means matched by her actions. On the contrary, incest is one of the lowest, most

---

[185] See this book, chapter 4. **Righteous Convert**, *Ruth's Declaration of Faith.*

despicable actions among the forbidden relations,[186] which is punished by excision.[187] Therefore, a spark of the soul of Lot's daughter had to reincarnate in order to get the opportunity to perform a righteous act, matching and encasing the purity of her original intention.

וַתֵּלֶךְ וַתָּבוֹא וַתְּלַקֵּט... (רות ב:ג)

"She went, and she came and she gleaned…"
(*Megillat Ruth* 2:3).

Ruth was the reincarnation of the daughter of Lot, as is hinted in this verse. "She went," in the way of people; "and she came," in a new incarnation, "and she gleaned" the fruit of her deeds, which she had done for the sake of Heaven. Ruth was gleaning the reward of Lot's daughter, who intended for the sake of Heaven, when she performed the deed with her father, in order to propagate the destroyed world.[188]

During the times of the Judges, there was a well-known tradition in Israel that one goodly spark in the future would come forth from Moav, in the merit of the daughter of Lot, whose intention was for the sake of Heaven. From this spark, the kingdom of David would be established.[189] For this reason, Naomi sent Ruth on a perilous and seemingly immodest mission: going down to the threshing floor in the middle of the night and lying down next to Boaz, a G-d-fearing man, whom she barely knew. Naomi's kidneys, (inner voice)

---

[186] *Vayikra* 18:7.
[187] Ibid. 29.
[188] Rabbi Moshe Alshich, *Megillat Ruth* 2:3.
[189] Rabbi Moshe Alshich, *Megillat Ruth* 1:8 quoting the following Midrash about Lot's daughter and her connection with the Mashiach.

ר' תנחומא משום רבי שמואל ונחיה מאבינו זרע ונחיה מאבינו בן אין כתיב כאן אלא ונחיה מאבינו זרע אותו זרע שהוא בא ממקום אחר ואי זה זה מלך המשיח: (מדרש רבה בראשית פרשה נא פסקה ח)

Rabbi Tanchuma in the name of Rabbi Shemuel, it stated, "…that we may preserve **seed** of our father." (*Bereishit* 19:32). It does not state, "that we may preserve **a son** of our father," only "seed" that comes from another place: This is the King Mashiach (*Midrash Bereishit Rabbah* 51:8).

advised her to persuade Ruth to go down quietly after Boaz had eaten and drunk, without letting him know of her lying down. This way, she would replicate the exact same manner in which Lot's daughter went quietly, without Lot being aware of her lying down. Then Boaz would know without any doubt that Ruth was the hidden spark from Moav, for the acts of the daughter reflected those of the mother. For this reason, Naomi told Ruth "come" – (וּבָאת) rather than "go" (וְהָלַכְתְּ), in order to allude to the language describing Lot's daughter.[190] A close reading and comparison between the texts describing Ruth's encounter with Boaz, and Lot's daughter approaching Lot, reveals several parallels.

Both Lot and Boaz had been drinking wine. Lot's daughters made Lot drink wine until he became so drunk that he was unaware of their actions. Boaz had also been drinking wine, but only until his heart had become merry,[191] without getting drunk. This is why the word וַיֹּאכַל – "had eaten" is mentioned before וַיֵּשְׁתְּ – "and drunk," interspacing the word "Boaz" between them, to indicate that Boaz's drinking was secondary to his eating. He remained fully aware of everything taking place between himself and Ruth. In this way he rectified Lot's drunkenness and lack of awareness.

In addition, the language of Scripture in the two stories have several linguistic parallels.

וַיֹּאכַל בֹּעַז וַיֵּשְׁתְּ וַיִּיטַב לִבּוֹ וַיָּבֹא לִשְׁכַּב בִּקְצֵה הָעֲרֵמָה **וַתָּבֹא בַלָּט** וַתְּגַל מַרְגְּלֹתָיו **וַתִּשְׁכָּב**: (רות ג:ז)

"When Boaz had eaten and drunk, and his heart was merry, he went to lie down at the edge of the heap of grain; and she **came** quietly, and uncovered his feet, and **lay** down" (*Megillat Ruth* 3:7).

---

[190] Rabbi Moshe Alshich, *Megillat Ruth* 3:4.
[191] The phrase טוב לב – *tov lev* – (merry heart) is used in connection with wine in II *Shemuel* 13:28, *Kohelet* 9:7, *Megillat Esther* 1:10.

וַתַּשְׁקֶיןָ אֶת אֲבִיהֶן יַיִן בַּלַּיְלָה הוּא **וַתָּבֹא**
הַבְּכִירָה **וַתִּשְׁכַּב** אֶת אָבִיהָ... (בראשית יט:לג)

"They made their father drink wine that night. And the first-born **came**, and **lay** with her father..." (*Bereishit* 19:33).

Comparing the text describing Lot's daughters with Ruth's lying down at Boaz's feet, we notice that the verses have two identical words, written in the exact same grammatical forms. וַתָּבֹא – "she came," and וַתִּשְׁכָּב – "and she lay down." In addition, the word בַּלָּט which means quietly (i.e. "she came quietly") is spelled exactly the same way as "to Lot," allowing an alternative reading as follows, "She [Ruth] came to Lot, and uncovered his feet, and lay down." Scripture thus clearly alludes to the fact that Ruth was the reincarnation of Lot's daughter, performing a replay of her original deed with Lot in order to rectify and elevate it. Boaz showed that he understood the hint by calling Ruth בְּתִי – "my daughter," twice. His immediate response to Ruth's allusion was, "Blessed be you of Hashem, my daughter. You have shown more kindness in the end, than at the beginning..."[192] "And now my daughter do not fear for whatever you say I will do to you, for all the gate of my people know that you are a woman of valor."[193]

Rescuing Oppressed Souls   להציל נשמות עשוקות

זֶה לְעֻמַּת זֶה עָשָׂה הָאֱלֹהִים... (קהלת פרק ז:יד)

"G-d has made one corresponding to the other" (*Kohelet* 7:14).

G-d in His infinite wisdom created the world with the contra point of good and evil, darkness and light etc. in order to

---

[192] *Megillat Ruth* 3:10.
[193] Ibid. 11.

ensure Free Will. Just as the obstacle course trains and advances the horse and rider, the opposing forces challenges us to actualize our full potential. Therefore, whenever we attempt to accomplish a holy mission the opposing negative forces in the world try to prevent us from reaching our goal. These negative forces that conceal the holy and are nurtured from it, are called *sitra achra* or 'the other side.'

There exist souls oppressed by forces of 'the other side,' which derive spiritual strength by subjugating them. It is almost impossible to rescue these souls from their oppression, for 'the other side' traps them to nurse sustenance from them. The only way to rescue these holy souls is by making them appear to be involved in unholy deeds. Then the opposing forces believe that these souls will remain in their power, even if they loosen their grip on them. By being involved in seemingly unholy deeds, the holy souls will be able to trick the forces of 'the other side' to let go of them. In this way, the holy souls can overcome their oppressors. This is why the souls of the tribes were born through two sisters: Rachel and Leah. Since the Torah prohibits marrying two sisters,[194] the forces of 'the other side,' were tricked into believing that the souls of the tribes would remain impure. The same is the case of the soul of Peretz, who was conceived through Tamar when she disguised herself as a harlot, as well as the soul of Ruth, the mother of Mashiach, who came from the impure land of Moav.[195]

King David described those who derided his seemingly impure lineage, because he descended from Ruth the Moabitess with the following verse from *Tehillim*, "O sons of men, how long will you turn my glory into shame?"[196] According to the Midrash,[197] David responded to their

---

[194] *Vayikra* 18:18.
[195] Malbim, *Megillat Ruth* 4:17, based on Arizal, *The Gate of Reincarnations,* Introduction 38.
[196] *Tehillim* 4:3.
[197] *Midrash Ruth Rabbah* 8:1.

disdain with the continuation of the psalm, "Commune with your own heart upon your bed."[198] With this verse, he was asking those who questioned his lineage, "Didn't you yourselves descend from the prohibition of two sisters?" Therefore, "be still,"[199] you have no argument against me. The elders at the gate blessed Boaz, saying, "May Hashem make the woman... like Rachel and Leah... and may your house be like the house of Peretz, whom Tamar bore to Yehuda..."[200] With these words they were alluding to the fact that the souls of his future offspring from Ruth would be redeemed from their unholy oppressors. This is similar to the souls of Rachel and Leah's children, and Peretz the son of Tamar. We can now understand why the soul of Mashiach had to travel through seemingly unholy conceptions, as this was the only way to rescue this holy soul from its spiritual oppressors.[201]

The Chafetz Chayim[202] explains the same idea regarding the conception of the House of David through Yehuda and Tamar. Yehuda did not turn voluntarily to be with Tamar; an angel forced him to turn toward her.[203] From here came the beginning of the House of David and King Mashiach, may he come soon! The lesson of the story is that 'the other side,' prevents the most high and lofty matters. Therefore, there is no other advice than to make the way crooked in order to appease 'the other side.' Events occurring in the straight way, the way of the Torah, would cause 'the other side' to accuse and deter the matter from being actualized. This principle also applies to Oved the grandfather of David, who came forth from Ruth the Moabitess.[204]

---

[198] *Tehillim* 4:5.
[199] Ibid.
[200] *Megillat Ruth* 4:11.
[201] Based on Malbim, *Megillat Ruth*, 4:11.
[202] Rabbi Yisrael Meir Kagan HaKohen, (1838-1933), Raduń Poland, influential halachist and ethicist, authored the halachic masterpiece *Mishnah Berurah*, and *Guard your Tongue*, about the importance to refrain from evil speech.
[203] *Midrash Bereishit Rabbah* 85:8.
[204] The Chafetz Chayim on the Torah, *Parashat Vayeshev*.

Whereas the intention of Lot's daughter, but not her action, was holy; the opposite is true regarding Yehuda, whose intention was all but holy when he thought Tamar was a prostitute. Nevertheless, unknowingly to himself, his action turned out to be the holy deed of *yibum* with Tamar, which produced Peretz, the ancestor of the Davidic dynasty. Yet, the lack of proper intention in Yehuda's action needed rectification. Boaz, the reincarnation of Yehuda, rectified his lack of pure intention.

בחינת בועז הוא בחינת יהודה ממש שהוא
המלכות הנקר' עוז לעמו יתן וזהו בו עז ומחלון
וכליון הם ער ואונן, ועובד בא לעבוד את
האדמה ולהסיר הקוצים מעליה לתקן הכל:
(לקוטי תורה, פרשת ויחי)

The aspect of Boaz is indeed the aspect of Yehuda, which is kingship, called *oz* as in, "Hashem gives strength [*oz*] to His people."[205] This is the meaning of [the name בֹּעַז/Boaz] –בֹּו-עָז/*bo oz*– "in him is strength." Machlon and Kiliyon were [the reincarnations of] Er and Onan, and Oved came to work the land and to remove the thorns from it, to rectify everything (Arizal, *Likutei Torah, Parashat Vayechi*).

When Boaz demonstrated extreme self-restraint by swearing to his *yetzer hara* (negative impulse) that he would not touch the woman who lay down at his feet in the middle of the night,[206] he was able to rectify Yehuda, who "turned to the 'prostitute' on the way." Although Boaz could have performed the mitzvah of *yibum* on the threshing floor then and there, he wanted to ensure that the mitzvah was completed in the highest way by offering the closest relative the opportunity first.[207]

---

[205] *Tehillim* 29:11.
[206] Rashi, *Megillat Ruth* 3:13.
[207] See *Megillat Ruth* 3:12.

Like Rachel & Leah   כרחל וכלאה

וַיֹּאמְרוּ כָּל הָעָם אֲשֶׁר בַּשַּׁעַר וְהַזְּקֵנִים עֵדִים יִתֵּן
הָשֵׁם אֶת הָאִשָּׁה הַבָּאָה אֶל בֵּיתֶךָ כְּרָחֵל וּכְלֵאָה
אֲשֶׁר בָּנוּ שְׁתֵּיהֶם אֶת בֵּית יִשְׂרָאֵל וַעֲשֵׂה חַיִל
בְּאֶפְרָתָה וּקְרָא שֵׁם בְּבֵית לָחֶם: (רות ד:יא)

"All the people that were in the gate and the elders, said,
'We are witnesses. May Hashem make the woman who
is coming into your house like Rachel and Leah, both of
whom built the house of Israel; and do valor in Efrat, and
become renowned in Beit-lechem'" (*Megillat Ruth* 4:11).

Arizal asks why the *Megillah* mentions "both of whom" since we
know that Rachel and Leah were two and not three. He answers
that Ruth includes both Rachel and Leah within her. Rachel and
Leah, just as Ruth and Orpah, were two sisters that converted.
Originally, Ruth corresponded to Rachel, and Orpah to Leah,
but when Orpah didn't convert, Orpah's good part was extracted
and given to Ruth. When Ruth became rectified, both Machlon
and Kiliyon became included in Oved, the father of Yishai.[208]

The Rama of Pano elaborates on this teaching by the Arizal.[209]
He holds that Ruth was the reincarnation of Rachel, whereas
Naomi was the reincarnation of Leah. This explains why Ruth
insisted to be buried with Naomi.[210]

נעמי מסוד לאה, ורות מסוד רחל, וזה שאמר הכתוב
ורות דבקה בה, שרחל מסרה סימנים ללאה, וזה
שאמרה רות ושם אקבר, כלומר לא כבראשונה
שלאה נקברה במערת המכפלה, ורחל נקברה בדרך
אפרת, ועובד שילדה אותו רות (והיה יהודה בן לאה,
לזה אמר הכתוב ילד בן לנעמי בן ממש: (כתבי
הרמ"ע מפאנו,   ספר גלגולי נשמות, אות נ:ה)

---

[208] Arizal, *The Gate of the Articles of the Sages, The Steps of Avraham Avinu.*
[209] Rabbi Menachem Azariya of Pano (a.k.a. Rama Mi-Pano), (1548-1620).
Italian Kabbalist, student of the Arizal.
[210] *Megillat Ruth* 1:17.

Naomi is from the secret of Leah, and Ruth is from the secret of Rachel. This is why Scripture stated "but Ruth cleaved to her,"[211] for Rachel transmitted the secret signs to Leah. This is why Ruth said, "And there I will be buried,"[212] meaning unlike previously, when Leah was buried in the cave of Machpelah, and Rachel was buried on the way to Efrat. Oved, whom Ruth gave birth to, was Yehuda, son of Leah. This is why Scripture stated, "a son was born to Naomi,"[213] a real son (The Rama of Pano, *The Book of Soul Reincarnations* p. 50).

After the elders and all the others who were in the gate had finished blessing Boaz and Ruth, the women blessed Naomi with the following blessing:

וַתֹּאמַרְנָה הַנָּשִׁים אֶל נָעֳמִי בָּרוּךְ הַשֵּׁם אֲשֶׁר
לֹא הִשְׁבִּית לָךְ גֹּאֵל הַיּוֹם וְיִקָּרֵא שְׁמוֹ בְּיִשְׂרָאֵל.
וְהָיָה לָךְ לְמֵשִׁיב נֶפֶשׁ וּלְכַלְכֵּל אֶת שֵׂיבָתֵךְ כִּי
כַלָּתֵךְ אֲשֶׁר אֲהֵבַתֶךְ יְלָדַתּוּ אֲשֶׁר הִיא טוֹבָה לָךְ
מִשִּׁבְעָה בָּנִים: (רות ד:יד - טו)

"The women said to Naomi, Blessed be Hashem, Who has not withheld a redeemer from you today. May his name be renown in Israel. He shall be a restorer of life to you, and sustain your old age; for your daughter-in-law, who loves you and is better to you than seven sons, has given birth to him'" (*Megillat Ruth* 4:14-15).

Rabbi Yosef Shani explains that these seven sons mentioned by the women are all of Naomi's children including those in her earlier incarnation as Bat Shua, Yehuda's wife. This includes: Er, Onan, and Shela, (born to Bat Shua and Yehuda), Peretz and Zerach, (Tamar and Yehuda's twins), who were the reincarnations of Er and Onan. They returned once again in

---

[211] Ibid. 14.
[212] Ibid. 17.
[213] Ibid. 4:17.

the reincarnations of Machlon and Kiliyon born to Naomi and Elimelech. The women understood that through the union of Ruth and Boaz, all of these seven previous descendants of Yehuda would become rectified and included in the soul of their son Oved, as a preparation of the all-inclusive soul of David, and Mashiach, the anointed one.

Rectification of the First Woman
תיקון האישה הראשונה

According to the Arizal, Ruth rectified that which Chava blemished in the days of the first man. Therefore it states, "The **woman** that comes..."[214] similar to the statement, "This one should be called **woman**."[215]

By eating from the Tree of Knowledge, Chava brought separations into the world. She created a gap between herself and Adam, between Adam and Hashem, between This World and the World to Come. The sin of eating from the Tree of Knowledge made it possible to separate between sexuality and holiness. Through the selfless mitzvah of *yibum*, Ruth unified the gap between sexuality and the holiness of mitzvot. By caring for the soul of her deceased husband, she repaired the breach between This World and the Eternal World of souls.

---

[214] *Megillat Ruth* 4:11.
[215] *Bereishit* 2:23. Arizal, *The Gate of the Articles of the Sages, The Steps of Avraham Avinu.* The above interpretation utilizes the *gezera shava*, a similarity of words or phrases occurring in different Torah verses from which we infer that what is expressed in the one, also applies to the other. In our case the analogy is made on the word "woman." *Gezera shava* is one of the thirteen methods of Torah interpretation cited by Rabbi Yishmael and is included in the daily prayer book as part of the Morning Prayer. It should be noted that citing and applying a *gezera shava* can only be done where the student received that specific comparison as a tradition from his teacher, and the teacher from his teacher, going all the way back to Mount Sinai. A student may not invent his own *gezera shava*.

The first woman brought mortality into the world by disobeying her Divine parent, Hashem. Conversely, Ruth performed the mitzvah of "Honor your father and mother"[216] to the highest degree. Therefore, she merited a very long life, which is the reward of honoring one's parents, "That your days may be long upon the land which Hashem your G-d gave you."[217] By cleaving to Hashem, through her devotion to Naomi, her mother-in-law, Ruth merited to live in the times of her great, great grandchild, King Shlomo. The Midrash testifies, "He [Shlomo] placed a chair for the mother of the king,"[218] to Ruth, the mother of Royalty.[219]

Chava blemished Hashem's Kingdom in the world and caused humanity to be expelled from G-d's Kingdom, the Garden of Eden. However, Ruth was able to restore royalty to Israel and ultimately, she will bring about the final Redemption and the return of Hashem's Kingdom to the repaired Garden of Eden, G-d willing speedily in our days!

---

216 *Shemot* 20:12.
217 Ibid.
218 I *Melachim* 2:19.
219 *Yalkut Shimoni* I *Melachim* 2:170, I *Divrei Hayamim* 4:10075; *Zohar Ruth* 1:5096; *Midrash Ruth Rabbah* 2:2.

About the Author

*R*ebbetzin Chana Bracha Siegelbaum, a native of Denmark, is founder and director of Midreshet B'erot Bat Ayin: Holistic Torah for Women on the Land. She holds a Bachelor of Education in Bible and Jewish Philosophy from Michlala Jerusalem College for Women, and a Master of Art degree in Jewish History from Touro College. Rebbetzin Chana Bracha creates curricula emphasizing women's spiritual empowerment through traditional Torah values. In 2010 she published her first book, *Women at the Crossroads: A Woman's Perspective on the Weekly Torah Portion.* The Rebbetzin, a gifted spiritual healer, also practices EmunaHealing through Emunah, tefilah and energy work. Chana Bracha has a married son and several granddaughters, and lives with her husband and younger son on the Land of the Judean Hills in Israel.

About the Artist

*E*lisheva Shira holds a Bachelor's degree from Parson's School of Design in N.Y.C. and a Master's of Fine Art from Suny New Paltz. She lives in Bat Ayin, Israel with her husband and five children. Elisheva's paintings express the beauty, warmth and spiritual simplicity of the life that surrounds her and the incredible wonder of the Land of Israel. You may contact her at eshira18@gmail.com, www.elishira.com.

Printed in the USA
CPSIA information can be obtained
at www.ICGtesting.com
LVHW040602090124
768402LV00065B/363